The *New* Nursing Homes

The *New* Nursing Homes

A 20-Minute Way to Find Great Long-Term Care

by Marilyn Rantz, RN, PhD;
Lori Popejoy, RN, GCNS;
and Mary Zwygart-Stauffacher, RN, PhD

Fairview Press • Minneapolis

Published by Fairview Press, 2450 Riverside Avenue, Minneapolis, Minnesota 55454.

Library of Congress Cataloging-in-Publication Data
Rantz, Marilyn J.
    The new nursing homes : a 20-minute way to find great long-term care
/ by Marilyn Rantz, Lori Popejoy, and Mary Zwygart-Stauffacher.
        p. cm.
    ISBN 1-57749-099-1 (pbk. : alk. paper)
        1. Long-term care of the sick. 2. Long-term care facilities--Quality
control. 3. Aged--Long-term care--Evaluation. 4. Consumer education.
I. Popejoy, Lori L. II. Zwygart-Stauffacher, Mary, 1955- III. Title.

    RA997 .R36 2001
    362.1'6--dc21   00-050381

First Printing: January 2001
Printed in the United States of America
05 04 03 02 01   7 6 5 4 3 2 1

Cover: *Cover design by Laurie Ingram Duren™*

For a free current catalog of Fairview Press titles, please call toll free 1-800-544-8207. Or visit our web site at *www.fairviewpress.org*.

*To residents and their families
who taught us so much
about quality of care and
what is truly important
about living in a nursing home.*

Contents

What, exactly, do nursing homes do? How do you find a good
one? Are there other options besides a nursing home? Learn
how to find the best care for yourself or your loved one.

How Could We Possibly Consider a Nursing Home?

In her own words, a daughter writes about her experiences
with community services, in-home help, nursing home
selection, and coping with change.

Do Your Homework

When shopping for a nursing home, take this questionnaire
along so you'll remember the most important things to watch
for. It's like visiting nursing homes with an expert at your side.

Chapter three: Interviewing the staff   55

Before making your choice, ask nursing home staff these key questions. We've provided samples of the answers you're likely to hear in high-quality facilities.

Chapter four: Interviewing families   85

You'll need one more source of information: people like you with relatives living at the nursing homes you're interested in. As with the staff interview in chapter 3, we've provided questions to ask along with samples of "good" answers.

The Money

Chapter five: Who will pay?   97

Payments may come from several sources, depending on your situation. Find out what to expect and how to negotiate the agencies and paperwork.

Moving In

Chapter six: Making it work   105

When a person enters a nursing home, everyone makes adjustments—residents, families, and staff. Find out what it's like working with staff, how to avoid common pitfalls, and when to speak up.

Help Nearby and Nationwide

Chapter seven: Ombudsmen, agencies, and web sites   127

Here you'll find a state-by-state list of ombudsman programs and state licensure and certification programs, as well as web sites to help you learn more about long-term care.

About the authors   165

Foreword

The decision to move into a nursing home can be heart-wrenching. With all the news headlines exposing the problems people have in getting appropriate and compassionate nursing home care, many individuals admonish their families to never put them in such a place. And family members typically agree. As a result, there is often little or no planning for what to do if a crisis occurs and a nursing home becomes the only option.

It can, in fact, be a good option. There are nursing homes in this country that provide good—even great—care. The trick is knowing how to find them. With *The New Nursing Homes*, you can quickly locate the better nursing homes in your area by taking a simple, twenty- to thirty-minute walk-through at different facilities. Even if your choice must be hurried, you'll find a number of things you can do to select a facility that meets your family's needs.

The New Nursing Homes is based on the "Walk-Through Observation Guide," a tool developed by Dr. Rantz and her colleagues to help nursing homes evaluate and improve their quality of care. When families began asking her help in finding a nursing home, Dr. Rantz knew it was time to bring this guide to the consumer. The response has been tremendous: "This guide really works! I don't know what I would have done without it. With some nursing homes, I just walked in, turned around, and walked out again, but I kept on looking. We found a wonderful place. Mom is getting the care she needs, the staff is good, and the food and activities are good. We know no place is perfect, but we think we have found a good one. Thanks for your help!"

This book will help you sort the good nursing homes from the bad, focusing on the positive and approaching the nursing home experience without fear. Still, it's a good idea to contact citizen advocacy groups in your state, or to check the web sites of consumer advocacy organizations, to be sure that the facility you are considering is not currently in financial trouble or accused of providing substandard care. No matter how well a facility is doing, a change of operator can alter a facility dramatically. There is no good way to protect against this, but if a facility is constantly changing ownership, it is not a good sign.

This consumer guide has the potential to help millions of people make better choices about long-term care. The better informed the public is, the less likely it is that poor or inadequate care will be tolerated, and the more likely it is that the nursing home industry will continue to improve its care.

JOANNE POLOWY, MSW, LCSW
Executive Director, Missouri Coalition for Quality Care

Preface

Nursing homes are changing. Consumers are demanding better services, more amenities, and above all, more caring and competent staff. In communities across the country, alternatives to nursing homes—senior housing, residential care, assisted living, adult daycare, homecare, and companion services—are becoming increasingly common. These competing alternatives are driving nursing homes away from traditional institutional models for long-term care toward more personalized homelike models.

This book is about teaching you how to recognize these "new" nursing homes—the ones, for example, that are embracing such new ideas for long-term care as the Eden Alternative, which emphasizes the quality of life of the residents and encourages the placement of pets, plants, and other homelike amenities in the rooms. Or Resident-Centered Care, which advocates decision-making by (rather than for) residents, as well as individualized care, personalized rooms, and a staff-focus on individual needs. These new nursing homes are the ones that are providing rehabilitation to help older people regain their strength and skills so they can return to independent living, and are offering holistic care for those who are terminally ill. In other words, these are the nursing homes that are providing the highest quality care.

The New Nursing Homes is based on over two decades of experience and original research. With the participation of numerous nursing home residents, their families, and the staff who serve them, we have developed a walk-through observation guide to help you quickly rate the quality of care in a nursing home after a twenty- to thirty-minute tour. This guide has been extensively field-tested in the United States and abroad. Included with the guide are sets of interview questions for you to use with nursing home staff and with family members of residents living in the nursing homes you visit, as well as corresponding sets of answers that you would ideally expect to hear in response.

Not only do we explain how to use the walk-through guide and interview questions to find the best nursing home care available, but we also discuss what nursing home care is (and should be), what long-term care options are available to consumers, how to finance long-term care, how to adjust to nursing home life, and where to find resources for additional information and services. To illustrate the decision-making process, we have included a story from a daughter about her family's experience when her mother and mother-in-law needed nursing home care.

Our hope is that the information in this book will help relieve you of the guilt and fear that often accompany the process of choosing a nursing home, and that your experiences with long-term care will be as positive and life-affirming as possible.

Acknowledgments

No project such as this is undertaken or completed without the support and hard work of many people. First, we want to acknowledge the support of our families and friends who have listened to our ideas and encouraged us to keep going.

Second, we must thank all the residents and their families and friends who contributed their time and experiences to our research, and helped us learn what quality in nursing home care truly means.

Next, we thank the many nursing home providers and staff who freely shared their invaluable insights with us.

Specifically, we want to thank Dale Smith for his marvelous editorial assistance; he transformed our academic prose into clear, everyday language. And we thank Janine Musick for her articles showcasing our work in *Family Money* magazine and the *Mizzou* alumni magazine; her encouragement helped us keep going.

We thank those consumers who have taken the time to read early and later versions of this manuscript; their guidance and insights were critical to this final product. We especially thank Joanne Polowy, Executive Director of the Missouri Coalition for Quality Care, who not only reviewed multiple versions, but also wrote the foreword for us.

Others who reviewed and provided wonderful letters of support and encouragement include Dr. Luther Chrisman, retired healthcare executive and AARP district coordinator in Nashville, Tennessee; Linda Golodner, president of the National Consumers League; Sarah Green Burger, executive director of the National Citizens' Coalition for Nursing Home Reform; Shawn Bloom, executive director of the National PACE

Association; Dr. William H. Thomas, founder of The Eden Alternative; and Lucille Vickerman, associate administrator of the Rock County Health Care Center in Janesville, Wisconsin.

And, finally, we thank all those who have worked closely with us, offering support and checking on our progress: Steven Miller, Bill Sheehan, Micheal Feinstein, Rose Porter, Priscilla LeMone, Roxanne McDaniels, Vicki Conn, Victoria Grando, David Mehr, Steve Zweig, and other members of the MU MDS and Quality Research Team.

Introduction

Bring up the topic of nursing homes with most people and you're likely to get a negative response. Lack of privacy, bad smells, poor food, inadequate staff, separation from friends and family, an unpleasant environment—these are some of the things that pop into people's minds. But this doesn't have to be the case. More and more, nursing homes are defying such stereotypes. These "new" nursing homes are moving away from the institutional, hospital-like settings of the past to offer more homelike, personalized care. In these new nursing homes, staff are more visible and attentive, family members are more involved, and facilities are cleaner and friendlier.

When we say "new nursing homes," we don't mean just those that have recently been built. Rather, we're referring to new attitudes about what nursing homes and other long-term care facilities can and should be. The age of the physical building is less important than the number of staff on site, the range of activities offered, the quality of personal and medical care, and the overall pleasantness of the environment. To put it another way, the "new nursing homes" are those progressive long-term care facilities that offer the highest quality care for their residents.

If you are reading this book, it's likely that you are in the process of looking for a nursing home for yourself or a loved one. You are probably asking yourself, "How do I find a good nursing home?" We try to help you answer this question by providing you with a simple, easy-to-use guide that allows you to evaluate any nursing home in a quick twenty- to thirty-minute walk-through. We also offer advice on how to adapt to a nursing home, how to finance your care, and how to locate resources both locally and nationwide. The advice we've assembled here is based on years of experience running nursing homes, on research that we and other professionals have conducted on the quality of care in nursing homes, and on conversations we've had with nursing home staff members and, more important, hundreds of consumers like you. Before we get too far into this advice, though, we need to explain some basics about nursing homes in particular and long-term care in general.

What exactly do nursing homes do?

NURSING HOMES are licensed to provide protective oversight of residents, as well as care and services that are needed when physical or mental impairments prevent older adults from living independently. Residents may need the services for a short-term stay of a few weeks or for a long-term stay of many months or years. Services include meals, laundry, assistance with personal care, nursing care, nursing supervision, medical care, recreational activities, and access to social workers and rehabilitation therapists.

Most nursing homes in the United States are owned and operated by proprietary (for-profit) businesses. Some are owned and operated by not-for-profit organizations like churches, religious groups, fraternal groups, and other non-profit agencies. A small percentage are operated by governmental agencies such as counties, districts, cities, or the Veteran's Administration.

Nursing home care may be paid for through personal funds, private insurance, public assistance, or some combination of these. Typically, long-term nursing home residents pay for the first months or years of care with their personal funds. When these funds are depleted, the Medicaid program kicks in and pays for the care as long as the person lives. Nursing home care for short-stay residents may be paid for by Medicare and other insurance while the resident rehabilitates from an illness or injury. We discuss the financing of nursing home care in much more detail in chapter 5.

What are my options for long-term care?

A NURSING HOME is not the only option for long-term care, nor is it always the best place for you or your loved one. From Meals-on-Wheels to skilled nursing, a variety of long-term care options exist for people in different situations. Selecting the best option depends on many factors: whether or not you have someone who can assist you in your home, how much personal and medical care you need, where you live, what community services are available, and what financial resources you have access to.

Some of the more common long-term care options in addition to nursing home care include senior services, homecare, live-in help, senior housing with services, subsidized senior housing, assisted living (or residential care), and board-and-care homes. A brief description of each of these options follows.

Senior services

A number of services are available to older adults around the country. Senior centers, for example, offer meal programs for those seniors who are able to come to a meal site. For those individuals who cannot come to the center site, many communities offer a Meals-on-Wheels program. Social events, health-promotion screenings, and clinical services are often available at senior centers as well.

In many communities, transportation is available for older adults who can no longer drive. This basic service is crucial in helping people remain in their own homes; without it, many individuals could not get to the grocery store, doctor's appointments, and other locations as needed. Although some communities will transport people in wheelchairs, many transportation programs require that clients be able to walk as well as get in and out of a van without much assistance. There may be a fee for transportation services, though costs are sometimes paid by public and private grants.

Some communities have private case management, or care coordination, available through private companies or community service agencies. Case managers help seniors and their families find local services, coordinate medical care, and obtain financial assistance.

Area Agencies on Aging, established by the Federal Older Americans Act, coordinate funding for senior services and centers. These agencies provide information about local services that help older adults remain healthy and independent in their own homes for as long as possible.

Senior services are funded in a variety of ways—by federal, state, and local sources. However, volunteers and active fundraising are essential for these services to meet the needs of older adults, many of whom cannot afford to pay for all the services they need to remain in their homes.

Homecare

After a hospitalization for illness or injury, many people hire a licensed homecare agency to help the individual recuperate at home. Generally, Medicare will pay for some homecare services. A nurse or physical therapist may come to the house to help manage the illness or to assist the individual in regaining his or her mobility and strength. A nursing assistant may come to help with bathing and personal care.

Homecare services also may assist with housekeeping, shopping, and other household chores that are difficult for some older adults. Sometimes, these services may be paid for by local, county, or state programs. Occasionally, they may be covered by private insurance. Frequently, however, the cost must be paid by the individual receiving the services or by the family.

Live-in help

Some homecare agencies and other placement agencies specialize in finding workers to live with older adults and provide basic housekeeping, meal preparation, and assistance with personal care. The fee—paid by the day out of personal funds—is less than typical homecare, and the workers are available around the clock. The older adults provide meals, a bedroom, and the use of other space in the house.

Senior housing with services

Some specially designed housing will offer health and personal care services as needed. Typically, the housing is an apartment or condominium development that includes conveniences to support independence, such as wheelchair access to bathrooms, showers, cabinets, power sources, and living spaces. Meals, activities, and transportation are usually part of the basic service package. As healthcare needs develop, the resident can purchase assistance with personal care, medication supervision, care coordination, and other services from a licensed homecare agency or another provider. Housing is paid for by personal funds; most other services are paid for through private insurance or personal funds.

Subsidized senior housing

Federal and state programs subsidize housing for older and disabled adults with low and moderate incomes. In subsidized senior housing, residents generally live independently in an apartment within a senior housing complex. Many facilities encourage volunteer programs and activities that foster socializing. Some also offer assistance with shopping, laundry, or other tasks. Individuals may hire a home health agency to help with healthcare or personal care needs; however, federal, state, and local funding usually will not cover the cost of these services. As an individual's care needs increase, nursing home placement becomes a viable alternative to the high cost of extensive in-home services.

Assisted living, or residential care

Assisted living, also called residential care, is a rapidly growing option for older adults who need some assistance with personal care, such as bathing, meals, laundry, medications, and housekeeping. In assisted living, residents generally live in private apartments while sharing meals and activities with the other residents.

Assisted living facilities are similar to nursing homes, except they provide less care and have fewer workers on staff. For example, in assisted living facilities, registered nurses are rarely on duty around the clock, and rehabilitation therapists may not be readily available. If you or your loved one will need nursing care or rehabilitation therapy, and you are considering assisted living, ask about the services provided. You may be able to use a home-care agency to supplement the care you receive in the facility, but you will likely have to pay for homecare services yourself. In this case, a nursing home may be a more suitable, less costly option. In fact, some assisted living facilities require residents to transfer to a nursing home if the need for care increases.

Licensing and funding vary from state to state, as do the definitions of residential care and assisted living. These facilities are often marketed to more affluent seniors, since the cost of assisted living is often paid from personal funds.

Board-and-care homes

Board-and-care homes are community-based group living facilities designed to meet the needs of older adults who can no longer live independently. These homes are typically large, private houses converted to accommodate eight to twenty people. Each person has his or her own bedroom. Residents share bathrooms, kitchens, living rooms, and porches with each other and, in some cases, with the owner or operator. Most of these homes provide some assistance with bathing, walking, toileting, and eating. In some states, public funding is available to residents; otherwise, personal funds must cover the costs. As with assisted living, regulations may require transfer from board and care to a nursing home if the resident's needs for care become advanced enough.

What long-term care options are available in my community?

BECAUSE REGULATIONS governing long-term care vary from state to state, and because availability of long-term care varies from community to community, you are going to have to do some investigation on your own to determine what your particular options are. Start with agencies that advocate for older adults, such as your local Area Agency on Aging, senior centers, healthcare organizations, community groups, department of social services, or public health department. (For a list of helpful state-by-state resources, see chapter 7.) Call and ask for guidance in obtaining listings of long-term care services. After just a few phone calls, you should have a good sense of what is available in your community. When talking to long-term care providers, be sure to ask exactly what services are offered, what they cost, how to apply for them, and whether they are restricted in any way, such as by income, age, or disability. You will also want to ask if you qualify for financial assistance. Don't forget that the U.S. Social Security Administration may be of assistance if you qualify for social security benefits.

What are the signs of quality care?

OUR RESEARCH ON nursing homes has led us to identify seven key aspects of quality care, which we label Home, Care, Family Involvement, Environment, Communication, Staff, and Central Focus.

Although these features have been distilled from research on nursing homes, they can be applied to other long-term care settings as well, especially assisted living, residential care, and board and care. And because many people will eventually need the services of a nursing home, if only for a short-term recuperative stay, the information that follows should prove useful no matter what long-term care option you choose.

Home

As its name implies, a nursing home should feel like a home, not like an institution or hospital. It should have the look and feel of an active place where people live and where they receive the care they need. It should be buzzing with life, hope, activity, and caring individuals. Each room should have plants and personal items so the resident can regard the room as his or her own. Local community groups should visit residents. A volunteer program should be active, involving children and pets and promoting a variety of group activities.

The mission of the nursing home should be obvious to all who live, work, and visit there. The top priority of the nursing home should be caring for residents and their families. Yes, nursing homes are businesses, and they need to watch the bottom line, but consumers say loud and clear that nursing homes should, first and foremost, take care of residents.

A most welcome refrain for all to hear is when residents say, "This is home now."

Care

A high-quality nursing home is one where the staff stays on top of the fundamentals of care, including:

- help with bathing, eating, and going to the bathroom;
- keeping residents' hair, teeth, and clothes clean;
- offering a variety of good food to eat in a sociable setting;
- helping people stay involved socially;
- arranging for medical help when necessary; and
- minimizing the occurrence of injuries and property loss. (These happen at one's own home, too, don't forget.)

Residents, families, and staff members should work together so residents get the special attention they want and need. One resident explained, "I want to know that the nurses are doing my care the way it should be done for *me*, not just for anybody. I have certain conditions and I know they need to be managed in certain ways so I don't get sick." Nursing home workers also should get to know each resident's history. One daughter remarked that "the staff should know that my dad was a farmer all his life and is likely to wake up very early because he milked cows for many years."

Residents need to be engaged in activities for their enjoyment and benefit. Good staff members make these activities fun and work to involve even those residents who are reluctant to join in. Look for variety: games, music groups, religious study groups, physical fitness programs, and current events discussions.

Family involvement

Good nursing homes encourage families to get involved with their loved ones' care. And family members say that spending time at the nursing home ensures that residents are fed, exercised, and medicated properly and in a timely fashion. When families work closely with staff members and really get to know them, they feel more confident that their loved ones are receiving the sort of personalized care they want them to have.

Getting involved often means hands-on work, such as washing clothes, bringing in favorite foods, or leading group activities. Some family members get so involved that they become political advocates for nursing home reform. Nursing homes are highly regulated by government agencies, and family members have testified before state and federal bodies about such issues as the need for increased recruitment, training, and reimbursement of nursing home staff. Highly involved volunteers may even join the board that operates the nursing home or advises the home's administrator about care issues.

Frequently, family members will form a family advisory or support group. Because families often experience similar issues related to nursing home care, they can be a great source of strength and support for each other. Families might also form networks to watch out for each other's relatives, something like a "neighborhood watch."

Environment

Consumers, families, and staff members all agree that a nursing home should be clean and odor-free. It should be spacious and not too noisy. It should feel like a pleasant place to live. The grounds around the facility should be inviting and accessible to residents, families, and community groups. The building should be well lighted, with lots of windows so residents can see outdoors. Furnishings and equipment should be functional and well maintained. This means that beds are low enough to minimize falls; tables are the right height for eating comfortably; and chairs are sturdy, with arms to help people stand up easily and safely. Floors should be nonslip and without glare. In general, the environment should be safe and free from obvious hazards.

Odor is a key indicator of quality. If you enter a nursing home and are overpowered by the odor of urine, feces, or perspiration, just turn around and walk out. Even if you have made an appointment, leave. This is not a place where you or your loved one would want to live. But don't despair—good nursing homes *are* out there. Keep looking.

Communication

Family members often mention communication—between families and the staff, between the staff and residents, between various members of the staff—as a crucial component of quality care. It's important that staff members hear—perhaps more than once—each resident's needs, likes, dislikes, and habits. There should be positive verbal and nonverbal communication between the staff and the residents. Good staff members will talk with residents and listen to what they have to say.

Staff

By now it should be clear that a good nursing home staff is perhaps the most important sign of quality care. Good staff members are responsive and compassionate. They are clean and well groomed. And they remain employed at the nursing home for several years. A well-trained, well-paid staff will generally stick around, and residents benefit from that continuity.

Nursing homes should be well staffed, with the same staff members caring for the same residents each day. Registered nurses must be closely involved in resident care to evaluate medical conditions and be alert to changes that need attention. Nurses who specialize in geriatric care should supervise, ensuring that residents get the care they need.

Central focus

"Central focus" means setting the right priorities. Good nursing homes focus not only on residents, their families, and the staff, but also on the community. We've already discussed residents, families, and staff; community involvement means participating in local events or politics, soliciting community support, or sponsoring educational programs such as those that teach healthy aging.

CONSUMERS AND NURSING HOME workers often have differing perspectives on the meaning of quality. To achieve true quality care, both customers and staff members need to imagine themselves in the others' position.

From the consumer's point of view, a good staff is paramount. As one family member said, "Without staff, nothing else is possible." Consumers have suggested that nursing assistants, who are the main providers of direct care to residents, should participate in orientation programs in which they spend a day or more as residents. Consumers want the staff to know how it feels to be given a shower in a shower chair, to be fed a meal, or to have to wait to be taken to the bathroom.

On the other hand, staff members see themselves working as hard as they can to do as much as they can for many people with different needs. They sometimes forget that residents see them as the center of their universe. It may serve you well to let staff members know how important they are to your family.

Sometimes, too, staff members are unaware of how beneficial family involvement can be. Families may need to seize the initiative to get more directly involved in their loved ones' care.

How do I evaluate the quality of a nursing home?

ONE WAY TO EVALUATE the quality of a nursing home is to examine its inspection history. Nursing homes are subject to close federal and state inspections, which are a matter of public record. Request the most recent state survey from any facility you are considering. But remember, the survey may be at least a year old—conditions may have changed considerably for the better or worse.

The government inspections, which occur at least annually, are meant to ensure that facilities meet minimum federal and state requirements regarding the building, sanitation, basic care and services, staffing, and administration. Although homes should have few violations, even a spotless inspection record does not guarantee a high-quality nursing home. Good care goes beyond the regulations. The inspection record is just one piece of information you will need to make an informed decision about long-term care.

Another document that might help you evaluate nursing home quality is a facility's "quality indicators" report (available for all Medicare- and Medicaid-certified nursing homes). This is a tabulation of the problems experienced by the residents at that particular nursing home. Quality indicators quantify such problems as weight loss, dehydration, skin breakdown, behavior problems, falls, and fractures. Scores for each nursing home are compared with those of other homes in the state. When visiting a nursing home, ask to see a copy of its most recent quality indicators report.

In chapter 7, you will find other sources to help you assess nursing home quality. We list numerous web sites that can help you locate government reports, government contact information, and consumer advocacy groups. We also list the ombudsman programs for each state. An ombudsman is a consumer advocate who helps investigate and resolve complaints made by nursing home residents, their families, or their friends. Perhaps the easiest way to locate your ombudsman is to call a local nursing home. The staff will know the ombudsman and how to contact him or her.

While information from government reports, consumer groups, and your ombudsman can be useful, **the only way you can be sure you've found a quality nursing home is to inspect it yourself.** Government reports will only tell you whether a nursing home meets minimum standards. Ombudsmen and consumer groups will only tell you if a nursing home has a history of problems or complaints. To learn about the positive aspects of a nursing home—to discover whether that home demonstrates the seven key signs of quality care—you must visit the facility yourself. And to make this visit as effective and efficient as possible, you need a guide that clearly defines what you should look for, how you should rate what you see, what questions you should ask, and what answers you should receive. Such a guide is provided for you in chapters 2, 3, and 4 of this book. We even provide evaluation forms that you can photocopy and bring along when touring different facilities. Using this book, you will be able to walk through any nursing home and rate its quality of care in a half hour or less.

1

One Family's Story

Before we get into the specifics of the walk-through, we'd like to offer an example of one family's experience making the nursing home decision. While every situation is unique, there are aspects of this experience that many families share. We hope this story reassures you that you are not alone as you make this very difficult decision.

A difficult decision

NURSING HOMES HAD always seemed negative places to me. My first experience with one was when my Brownie troop visited our leader's grandmother's home. We sang songs and gave the residents May baskets we had made. Even though we were doing a good thing and everyone was friendly and fussed over us because we were cute, we were frightened and glad to get out. I remember being told that it was a character-building event, that we would learn from it, and that the people who lived there were courageous and deserved our sympathy.

That was probably part of the reason why I took groups to nursing homes after I grew up and became a mom, a teacher, and a leader for lots of church-related activities. Usually we visited nursing homes to see elderly members of our congregation who were living there. My vacation Bible school classes visited to sing songs, recite verses, and put on puppet shows. We always received a lot of applause and cheers, and lots of cookies and juice.

I thought we were there to cheer up the residents, to brighten their dreary days. I felt sorry for the people who had to live in the nursing homes, and, most likely, without intending to do so, I communicated that feeling to my charges. No one that I knew well actually lived in one. I was certain that nursing homes were all terrible places, even though things looked all right when we were there. I knew I would never want anyone I loved to live there—certainly and especially not my mom.

Last summer, my husband and I did the unthinkable. After years of dealing with their declining health and growing dependence, we admitted both our beloved mothers to the same nursing home. Circumstances made it necessary. It was hard on all of us, but it was the best thing we could have done—for Steve and me, for my father-in-law, for our children and grandchildren, and, most of all, for our mothers.

My mom

MY MOM HAS ALWAYS been sickly. I grew up as an only child. I always worried about her, especially since my dad died when I was seven. Mom had to work, something most other moms didn't do at that time. I was a latchkey kid and was used to coming home to fix my own lunch. After I'd eaten, I would wash the dishes and read until it was time to return to school. I felt independent and resourceful. After school, however, it would be getting dark and my self-confidence would vanish with the daylight. I was always afraid that something terrible would happen to Mom on her way home from work—that the bus would career around the corner and hit and kill her, or that someone would rob the bank next door to the newspaper office where she worked and shoot her. If she died, I'd be alone, really alone.

More often than not, though, my mom would be ill and have to stay home from work. Then I would eagerly come home at lunch and after school. Her illnesses ranged from viruses to pleurisy to female problems to heart problems. She'd tell me about the illnesses she'd had—about how she'd had rheumatic fever as a teenager and missed most of her junior year. She'd still graduated in the top five of her class, but her heart was permanently affected by the illness.

I worried about her all the time—when I went to pajama parties, when I went to camp, when I went on church youth trips, when I went away to college, and when I got married and moved four hundred miles away. When she retired from her newspaper job, she moved to the same city where Steve and I lived with our three children. She had a condo across town in a retirement community. There would be infrequent but disturbing emergencies, and I would go to take care of her. Everyone but me understood that she would become "ill" whenever she wanted something or disapproved of something.

After our children graduated from high school and went to college, and after Steve received a promotion, we decided to move to a new community. We began building our dream house about forty miles south of where we were living. That was when Mom's illnesses became more frequent and severe. She disapproved of the move.

Her blood pressure, which had been kept in check for about twenty years by a daily pill, was now soaring to alarming heights. Every time her doctor gave her a new medicine, she became violently ill and would have to be taken to the emergency room.

By the time our new home was completed and our old home was sold, we realized that we would have to take her with us. She was always sick. Our new pastor told me that he thought she wanted to move in with us. I was resentful, but Steve wasn't surprised at all. We discussed the matter and knew that we did not want her to live with us; so we found her a duplex down the block from us.

Getting support services to help

As MY MOM'S HEALTH—including her eyesight—worsened, she began to require more assistance at home. I set up as many programs as possible for her through our state's department of human services. One of the programs was a crisis line, a service that provided emergency aid for elderly people through our local hospital. This involved my mom wearing a small transmitter around her neck at all times. If she fell or needed help and could not get to a phone, all she had to do was press the button on the transmitter, and this would signal to an operator that my mother needed help. The hospital would then try to call my mom, and, if they couldn't reach her, they would call us or send an ambulance to her home.

Other helpful programs included our community's Meals-on-Wheels program, a service that Steve and I had worked with as volunteers through our church. Since Mom was losing her eyesight, a person from Lighthouse for the Blind would visit her once a month. She would assess Mom's needs, and provide her with tools to help her in her daily life: a cooking timer with huge numbers, a powerful lamp, magnifiers, a talking watch, a special radio with a radio station for the vision-impaired, a four-track tape player for playing tapes of books, and a record player for playing recordings of magazines. These services were offered free of charge to my mother.

Often, I hired friends, neighbors, and church members to help Mom. They would come in during the day while we were at work to check on her and stay with her if she were especially ill. We also hired someone to clean her apartment twice a month.

Steve's mother

MY HUSBAND STARTED looking at nursing homes for his mother at least a year and a half before I did. His mother has rheumatoid arthritis. For a long time, she toughed it out, cleaning, cooking, and doing her community work. But it was taking more and more time and more and more medication for her to accomplish these things.

Steve's mother had always taken care of her home and family. She was the world's greatest cook—at least her family, neighbors, and friends all thought so. Whenever someone was sick, she would make a huge pot of soup and a large loaf of bread to take to them. For every potluck, bake sale, or ham dinner, our church could always count on Mother. But as time went by, it became increasingly difficult for her to take care of things. Dad, who had always been the breadwinner, was puzzled and sometimes angry. He believed that she just wasn't trying hard enough.

Rheumatoid arthritis is a slow and horrifyingly progressive disease. Mother never complained; she didn't want to worry us, even when her condition worsened to the point that she couldn't walk on her own. Finally, she couldn't pick up a glass or fork, or comb her hair.

Steve came back from his nursing home searches depressed and angry. He spoke of the bad smells in the homes he had looked at and the cries of the people who needed attention. Some workers were flush-faced and scurrying, overwhelmed by their responsibilities. Other employees were lethargic and appeared to ignore the people who needed assistance.

We worried about Dad. We feared that all of their money would go toward Mother's care, and that Dad would have nothing left for himself. Plus, Dad was demanding and had no idea how to cook or manage a home. We knew that it wouldn't work for Dad to live with us, or, for that matter, with any of Steve's brothers and sisters. It seemed wrong to feel this way, but we all agreed that this was so. All of us had jobs and families.

Finally, Steve found a good "senior housing facility." Steve's dad could live in a supervised setting called assisted living. In the same complex was a nursing home in which Steve's mother could stay. Dad would have his own room, his clothes would be washed, clean sheets and towels provided, and he could eat every meal with Mother and visit her as often as he wished. They could watch movies and eat popcorn in the multipurpose room every Friday night. There would be card games and bingo several times a week; these were things they loved to do. There was one problem, however: Steve's parents refused to go. This was their home; this was where they would stay.

Their decision to stay home made it hard for everyone in Steve's family. We were all taking turns washing clothes, cooking, and cleaning. Unfortunately, we were also arguing about who was doing the most for Mother and Dad. We'd never been this angry with each other before, we'd always been close. Some family members who had promised to do things didn't follow through. It was so hard for some of them to see Mother so crippled, they just wouldn't show up when it was their turn to help. And Steve's parents wouldn't "tattle" on them.

Steve's mother was receiving a few home services from Medicare: a social worker, a visiting nurse three times a week, a therapist once a week, and a bath lady three times a week. But they were there for only an hour at a time.

We were concerned about the times when no one but Dad was home with her. Mother couldn't walk to the bathroom. We found out from a neighbor that she would call and call for Dad to take her. He would either be asleep or ignore her. She would end up wetting herself. She had sores that were becoming infected. She couldn't wipe herself after she went to the bathroom, and Dad refused to help her. He would not change her clothes, and she often wore the same outfit for days. We discovered that he was only feeding her one meal a day. He would go out for his meals—leaving her alone for an hour or more—and bring her back a sandwich.

Things weren't going well, but it took us a long time to understand that. We aren't stupid, ignorant, or cruel. We are nice, hard-working people. But as uncomfortable and unhappy as Mother was, she never complained. Both she and Dad told us they were doing fine. Only over time did it become apparent that Steve's mother would die if she didn't get better care.

Live-in help for Steve's mother

STEVE INVESTIGATED live-in homecare. We had heard good things about one agency from neighbors and acquaintances, and we decided to contract its services. Steve and his brothers and sisters cleaned out the spare bedroom so the homecare worker would have a place to stay. We had to gather stuff that had accumulated over decades, pack it in boxes, and store it in the basement of our house.

Steve's mother was worried that their possessions would be lost or damaged. Dad was angry because he didn't want some stranger living in his house. Steve, being the eldest of his siblings, had to be the tough guy. Although it was difficult to do, he told his Dad that Mother needed to be taken care of and that Dad hadn't been doing a good job of it. Because Dad had refused to go to the senior housing facility, we were going to have to get a live-in caregiver for Mother. Steve then said the words that would become the family's motto in the hard months and years ahead. "This isn't what you want, but it is what you need. We love you and we are going to do what you need, even if you get mad at us." Even now, Steve will shake his head and say, "I never thought I'd talk to my father that way." And even now, I must keep reminding him that we really are doing what they need.

We called the agency and hired a woman from Romania named Deanie, who stayed with Mother and Dad for about nine months. Deanie did a good job. She kept Mother clean, changed her clothes, gave her nutritious food to eat, made her do the exercises recommended by the visiting nurse and therapist, and got rid of her sores. But it was hard for Steve's parents to adjust to another person living in their house, and she and Dad argued constantly. This was his home and his wife, and he knew what was best for Mother. But Deanie also wanted what was best for Mother; she was herself the mother of two sons and had formerly held an executive position in Romania. Deanie was used to giving orders. But she wasn't used to cooking, particularly American dishes. Dad hated her cooking.

Every two weeks, Steve or another family member would take Deanie to the train station so she could have two days off. During those two days, family members would take turns staying with Mother and Dad.

Taking care of Steve's mother was hard work, both physically and emotionally. Although Mother was a tiny woman, it was difficult to lift, dress, and wash her. Taking her to the toilet was very strenuous, especially for the females in the family. Wiping and cleaning her was not a particular problem for the women and girls, but it provoked extreme discomfort in her sons. They did it anyway, because it was something that had to be done.

Because of Deanie, Mother gained weight, and her sores and infections healed. We knew that Dad and Deanie had some loud and bitter fights, but Mother was better off for Deanie being there. Eventually, however, Deanie decided to return to Romania, and the agency brought in a replacement named Sally.

Sally had been a math teacher in the country of Georgia, which was formerly a part of the Soviet Union. She was a widow with two grown sons. She told us that her sons were doctors but were having a hard time making enough money to support their families. Sally stayed for three months. She got along very well with Dad. She cooked the sort of food he liked, was an excellent caregiver for Mother, communicated well with the family, and, in her own quiet way, managed things quite well.

When Sally suddenly married a math professor from a nearby university, she sent her niece Marta in her place so that we wouldn't be left without anyone to take care of Mother. But it quickly became apparent that Marta was not taking care of Mother as well as the two previous caregivers had. Mother's sores returned, and she complained that Marta would leave her for long periods of time to go for walks or drives in her car. Marta was not a good cook, and the dishes were left undone for long periods of time. The sinks, bathtub, and toilets were only cleaned every two weeks when a family member stayed over during Marta's days off. Mother had always been so neat, and the messiness of the house disturbed her. We tried several times to get Dad and Mother to fire her—the agency would have provided a replacement on a day's notice—but they were used to her and refused to do it. Marta was by far the strongest caregiver they had had. She could pick Mother up and carry her with ease, something even her sons could not do.

My mom ... things getting worse

IN THE MEANTIME, my mom was having more health problems, the most debilitating being the loss of vision due to macular degeneration. Her blood pressure was out of control. My husband and I took turns staying with her. We often had to rush her to the emergency room in the middle of the night.

Because of the needs of our parents, Steve and I sometimes went days at a time without seeing each other. We were taking as much time off work as we could. Thankfully, the kids were grown, but one or the other of us was often unable to attend family gatherings because of the demands of providing care for our parents. On holidays, I usually stayed with my mother and didn't get to see the rest of the family. Mom was always ill; any small upset would send her blood pressure shooting up if I wasn't there to take care of her.

I often got only one to three hours of sleep a night. When I wasn't teaching, I was with my mom or taking care of my own house: cleaning, paying our bills, and sharing a few moments with Steve. I was drinking an alarming amount of coffee just to stay awake. As I look back, I realize how stressed and exhausted both Steve and I were as we struggled to care for our mothers.

Mom was hospitalized that Thanksgiving. After she was released, Medicare homecare workers began coming out to assist her. Like Steve's mother, Mom had a nurse, a physical therapist, a bath lady, and a social worker. She was also assigned an occupational therapist because of her decreasing eyesight. She was blind now except for a small area at the rim of her left eye. Then, just two weeks before Christmas, she developed sciatica. The sciatic nerve in her back was pinched, and she was in terrible pain. The doctor was careful about giving her pain pills because of her other medications. Through all of this, she kept insisting that she was independent and didn't want a stranger living in her apartment, and definitely did not want to go to a nursing home.

Holidays ... more trouble

FOR YEARS, STEVE AND I had hosted holiday dinners at our house, but my sisters-in-law took pity on us and said they'd host both Thanksgiving and Christmas that year. We were grateful; we couldn't have done it.

Probably the hardest day for me was Christmas day. I had had the week before Christmas off from school. Even though I had been at Mom's house most of the time, Steve and I managed to decorate the house and wrap the presents. I had prepared several dishes to take to our family dinner (mostly in Mom's kitchen) and left them in our refrigerator. As usual, Steve and I had plans to set up some of the toys for our grandchildren to see as they entered the house. There's nothing like seeing their surprised, joyful, wondering little faces when they see the huge tree and all the presents! It's a grandma's dream.

Because Mom was sick, she refused to come to the family celebration or even over to our house for a short time. Even worse, she refused to let me go. I did not get to watch my grandchildren discover their Christmas gifts. Steve called me on the phone, and, as he took pictures, I listened to my daughter describe what was happening. I stayed with Mom all day while everyone else, including Steve's parents, celebrated at his brother's house.

I was angry and ashamed that I hadn't been there when the kids arrived. I resented the fact that I had missed Christmas with the rest of our family. I had so looked forward to seeing my grandsons react to the toys we had set out in front of the Christmas tree. But I was a monster, wasn't I, to want that when my mom needed me?

Christmas crisis

LATER THAT NIGHT, exhausted and emotionally drained, I left my mom sitting comfortably in her chair and came home to have a little bit of Christmas with Steve. I'd taken her to the bathroom, gotten her a drink, and told her not to move until I came back in a couple of hours.

Steve and I exchanged gifts, drank some eggnog, and fell asleep in front of the fireplace in each other's arms. We were awakened by the telephone. It was the crisis line calling to say that Mom had fallen at her duplex. It had been an hour and a half since I had left her. We raced over, got her up, and put her to bed. She had fallen on soft carpeting and was unharmed. Later, we learned that she may have had a mild stroke. I stayed with her until the day before New Year's Eve.

I was haunted by the fact that I had left Mom alone. I remembered how Marta had been leaving Steve's mother, and I felt that I was just as bad. Plus, lack of sleep and overwork were causing me to feel depressed and hopeless. I realize now that I was making unrealistic demands on myself. At the time, though, all I could think was that I was a monster, a bumbling, fumbling, inept monster who couldn't get anything right. I had to get some help. Maybe if someone else could take care of Mom, I could get some much-needed sleep, catch up on my work, get back to being close with my husband, and feel normal about myself again.

Live-in help for my mom

WE CALLED THE SAME homecare agency that we had used for Steve's mother. The agency sent us a woman from Ukraine named Tara. I was so relieved. It was wonderful to have someone who knew how to take care of an elderly person. I gave Tara a list of phone numbers, baked a casserole, cleaned the apartment, and did everything else that I thought might help. Steve dragged me home and insisted that I go to bed. I slept pretty much straight through for two days. When I wasn't sleeping, I graded papers and made lesson plans. I called Mom two times each day.

Then one day Mom said that she was scared of Tara because she was so gruff. That same day the visiting nurse came, discovered that Mom's blood pressure was sky-high, and strongly suggested that I fire Tara. I did, and, within hours, the agency sent Suzy, a woman from Poland, for an interview. Suzy appeared to be very competent. Unfortunately, Mom had a stroke after Suzy had been there for only two days. I was present when the stroke occurred. The bath assistant had just given Mom her shower and I was setting her hair. Suddenly the whole left side of her face drooped like it had melted; she tried to tell me that her hands were tingling, but only gibberish came out of her mouth. I immediately called 911. It was the day before school was scheduled to start. I stayed at the hospital all night. Then, because Mom was out of danger, I went to work the next day.

While Mom was hospitalized, we continued to pay Suzy. Friends would pick her up and take her to the hospital, where she kept Mom company during the day. Steve and I would visit Mom after work, then take Suzy back to Mom's apartment. Mom surprised the doctor and hospital staff by recovering very quickly. She was home in a week and a half, and Suzy took charge of her. Things were good. I got enough sleep, I could be at home, I could spend time with my husband, I got to see other family members occasionally. We went to Mom's apartment twice a day, before and after work, to visit and to bring them what they needed from the grocery store and pharmacy. On Suzy's days off, I would stay with Mom.

As was the case with Steve's parents, Mom's savings were dwindling rapidly. In fact, hers would run out before theirs. We needed to get Mom into a nursing home on private pay as soon as possible. When her money ran out, she'd be eligible for Medicaid. We wanted to place her quickly because we were afraid that it would be harder to get her into a nice home if she were already on Medicaid.

The nursing home search

WE BEGAN AGAIN TO look for nursing homes. But every time I visited one, I ended up crying in the administrator's office. How could I think of doing this? My mother, in a nursing home? All nursing homes are awful, aren't they?

Well, some of them are. I noticed many of the things that Steve had reported from his earlier research. The smells were the first clue that things weren't good. Also, the workers in many of the homes seemed overworked and overwhelmed.

But there were nice places, too—places where I could sense a genuine affection between the residents and workers. I encountered a nurse in one home patiently explaining to a resident about the change her doctor had made in her medicine. I saw workers and residents sharing a laugh together. I saw a resident hug an aide and call her "my girl" and "honey." I saw residents walking together arm in arm, one frail little woman helping another with poor eyesight to the dining room under the unobtrusive but watchful eye of an aide or nurse.

One of our nieces, who is a nurse, gave us a list of things to look for when we visited different nursing homes. This gave us definite, concrete signs to watch for, making the process less emotional and more rational.

The home we had looked at for Steve's parents was now full, so there was no room for my mom. Friends from church told us about a good home that was quite a bit farther away. We worried about placing my mom so far away, but we also wanted to get the best facility we could. We went to see it. It really was better than the one we had set our hopes on. She could have a room of her own. There were lots of activities. The people were kind. It didn't smell.

We asked the employees how long they had worked there. We noticed that residents had a few pieces of their own furniture in their rooms, along with family pictures, afghans, stuffed animals, plants, and other homey things. Several people invited us into their rooms to look around, and they always ended up telling us about their family members in the pictures. We spent a lot of time talking to the people who lived there because we thought it was the best way to find out what the place was really like. We learned that we could bring the family dog and cat whenever we came to visit. Pets were not only allowed but encouraged, with the understandable exception that they couldn't be brought into the dining room. We found out which beauticians the residents preferred and what days were best for scheduling an appointment. We found out what soaps worked best in the whirlpool baths. We were told about church services, about the Friday night movies with popcorn, about the resident who gave occasional piano concerts, about the excellent laundry service. And everyone said the food was great, especially the raisin cream pie.

Explaining to my mom, it's time

WE TOOK MOM TO visit the nursing home on Suzy's day off. She didn't like it, of course. We explained about her diminishing funds, and she countered with several different plans to keep her apartment, all of which were impractical. As lovingly as possible, and with many tears, I explained that we could no longer take care of her the way she needed to be taken care of. Our youngest daughter was planning to get married in September, and I needed time to do the million things that the mother of the bride must do. I couldn't prepare for the wedding, manage my home, teach school, and take care of Mom. We went ahead and made arrangements to move Mom to the home in June, the earliest that we could get her in.

Coincidentally, Suzy announced at this time that she would be leaving our employment in June. I felt that this was evidence of God's will. It was amazing to me that the day before Suzy planned to return to Poland was the day Mom was scheduled to move to the nursing home. It helped me to feel that we were doing the right thing; I was at peace with our decision.

Steve's mother ... it's time, too

IN THE MEANTIME, Steve's mother's sores were making her increasingly uncomfortable. A nurse we knew said that people could die from pressure sores if they became infected. That lit a fire under us. We went back to the home we'd chosen for my mother to ask about Steve's mother getting in there, too. The floor she would need was filled except for a private room that cost $15 more a day. We said we would take it, with the understanding that Mother would be put into a semiprivate room as soon as one was available.

Living again

BOTH OF OUR MOTHERS are doing well. Since moving to the home, my mom's life has been saved several times. When her blood pressure goes up, the medical staff there react immediately. A staff member told me that just last week my mom was talking with a brother and sister who were searching for a nursing home for their mother. She invited them into her room, told them why she had arranged the room as she had, and gave them advice about the beauty shop and food choices. She confided that she hadn't wanted to come to the home, but that she now understood it was necessary. She probably never will tell me this, but I feel better knowing that she said it.

Steve's mother is being treated by a physical therapist for her arthritis. She has regained enough use of her hands that she can feed herself again. Her sores have healed, and she is beginning to take a few steps. Both of our mothers have made new friends. Dad is lonesome sometimes, but he is also freer to visit with his friends more often. He comes to the nursing home to visit Mother and eat with her at least three times a week. We don't worry all the time, and our visits are pleasant. As before, some of Steve's family visit often; others make excuses. It isn't as necessary for all of us to take turns visiting, however, because we are not providing direct care for either woman. Now, professionals who know what they are doing are taking care of them.

I wish I could say that we did everything right and that everything is perfect. But things are never perfect. Still, we did the best we could, and our mothers are now well taken care of. Our family squabbles less, and, most important, we have our lives back again.

2 The Walk-Through

In the introduction, we explained the seven signs of quality nursing home care and suggested some resources for locating such care in your community. The next step is to visit and compare facilities. This may be one of the most difficult choices you'll have to make, so shop around. You can expect to visit several nursing homes before making your decision.

Start by looking at the nursing homes in your community— you may find the best one close to your home. That convenience is great if you can find it. If you are not satisfied with the nursing homes in your community, keep looking. Go to the next community. It is better to be farther from home where the care is good than to settle for substandard care close by. We have talked to many families who say they are much happier with their loved one in a really good nursing home, even if it is farther away, than when they experienced poor care in another home and were constantly worried if the residents were getting the help they needed.

When considering a facility, call and make an appointment with the admissions staff for a tour. Or, if you like, start by just going to the home to observe and talk with some of the staff. Then, when you are ready, explain to a staff member that you are looking for a nursing home and ask if someone can take you for a tour.

Because a tour is your best opportunity to evaluate a nursing home, you need to know *exactly* what to look for during the walk-through. On pages 42 to 54, you will find a detailed questionnaire to guide you. It tells you specifically what to watch for and how to judge quality of care. Make as many copies of this questionnaire as you need, and bring a copy along on every tour. Then, after visiting several facilities, you can look back on your notes and compare.

The walk-through questions are based on years of research with consumers and providers of nursing home care. The questionnaire has been tested in many nursing homes and assisted living facilities, so we're confident that it will help you in your search.

Before answering the walk-through questions, we recommend that you tour the facility for twenty to thirty minutes during business hours. Walk through living spaces, hallways, and areas generally available to the public. (If you have difficulty scoring a particular item, you may need to revisit some

Key Points to Remember
When Choosing a Nursing Home

Residents should be clean, groomed, dressed, up and about, and involved in activities both indoors and outdoors.

Staff members should be clean; groomed; friendly; active; helpful; and, most of all, caring.

Interaction between staff members and residents should be cordial and humane, even when residents are confused. Both staff members and residents should treat each other with respect and dignity.

Facilities should be clean, uncluttered, well maintained, and well lighted.

The atmosphere should be calm, pleasant, and homelike.

areas before you leave.) Ask yourself, "Is this a place where I or my family member will feel comfortable living?" Be a good observer; think about what you see, hear, smell, feel. Listen to your senses and trust your judgment.

A note about choosing your answers: The multiple-choice answers range from 1 to 5, with 1 being the worst and 5 indicating the best quality care. Be sure to answer every question that applies to that facility. When you are finished, add up the scores for each question, then divide by the number of questions answered. This will give you a "quality score" ranging from 1 to 5. (Again, 1 indicates the lowest quality of care; 5 indicates the highest.)

After touring several nursing homes, go to the summary sheet on the opposite page. You can use this space to compare quality scores and other pertinent information before choosing a nursing home for yourself or your loved one.

The nursing home tour is only part of the evaluation process. You'll also want to interview staff members and talk to families with loved ones living in that facility. So, in addition to the walk-through questions, we recommend you bring the questionnaires from chapters 3 and 4 each time you tour a facility. Together, the three questionnaires will give you a complete picture of life in a particular nursing home.

Note:
The questionnaire beginning on page 42 is adapted from "Observable Indicators of Nursing Home Care Quality, Version 5.1 for Consumers" © 1998, 1999 MU MDS and Quality Research Team.

Summary Sheet

Facility	Location	Contact Information	Visit Date	Quality Score	Notes

The Walk-Through Questions

Facility _____ Date _____ Time _____

1. Did staff members and residents have friendly conversations?

1	2	3	4	5
Most did not	*A few did*	*Some did*	*Many did*	*Most did*

2. When staff members talked to residents, did they call them by name?

1	2	3	4	5
Most did not	*A few did*	*Some did*	*Many did*	*Most did*

3. Did residents and staff members acknowledge each other (through smiles, eye contact, touch, etc.) and seem comfortable with each other?

1	2	3	4	5
Most did not	*A few did*	*Some did*	*Many did*	*Most did*

4. Did residents and staff members interact with each other in positive ways (through conversation, humor, touch, eye contact, etc.)?

1	2	3	4	5
Most did not	*A few did*	*Some did*	*Many did*	*Most did*

5. Other than at naptime or bedtime, were residents up and out of bed?

1	2	3	4	5
Most were not	*A few were*	*Some were*	*Many were*	*Most were*

6. Were residents dressed and clean?

1	2	3	4	5
Most were not	*A few were*	*Some were*	*Many were*	*Most were*

7. Were residents well groomed (shaved, hair combed, nails clean and trimmed)?

1	2	3	4	5
Most were not	*A few were*	*Some were*	*Many were*	*Most were*

8. Were staff members visible? (There should be enough staff members on duty that, as you tour, you see them working about the nursing home.)

1	2	3	4	5
Rarely seen	Occasionally	Sometimes	Often	Very often

9. Were staff members seen actively caring for residents? (Staff should seem busy working with residents as you tour the nursing home.)

1	2	3	4	5
Rarely seen	Occasionally	Sometimes	Often	Very often

10. Were registered nurses (RNs) visible? (This is important, because registered nurses are needed to evaluate residents and see that they get the care they need. You may need to look at name badges of staff to identify RNs. This question may not apply to assisted living or residential care facilities.)

1	2	3	4	5
Rarely seen	Occasionally	Sometimes	Often	Very often

11. Did registered nurses (RNs) seem to know the residents well enough to direct their care? (You may need to ask staff members to answer this question. This question may not apply to assisted living or residential care facilities.)

1	2	3	4	5
Did not	Occasionally	Sometimes	Often	Very often

12. Did staff members appear clean and well groomed?

1	2	3	4	5
Most did not	A few did	Some did	Many did	Most did

13. Did staff members appear caring (compassionate, warm, kind)?

1	2	3	4	5
Most did not	A few did	Some did	Many did	Most did

14. Did staff members appear to treat residents with respect and dignity?

1	2	3	4	5
Most did not	A few did	Some did	Many did	Most did

15. Were a variety of activities available for residents with different capabilities? (Look for posted schedules, calendars, etc.)

1	2	3	4	5
Rarely seen	A few were	Some were	Many were	Lots were

16. Did the staff help residents with food and fluids? (Generally, most residents need frequent help and encouragement with food and fluids throughout the day, not just at mealtimes.)

1	2	3	4	5
Rarely	Occasionally	Sometimes	Often	Very often

17. Were residents independently moving about the facility, with or without canes, walkers, splints, wheelchairs, or other assistive devices? (Generally, you should see some residents up and moving about the nursing home. It is important to encourage older adults to be as active as possible. Maintaining or regaining mobility is a primary goal for most residents.)

1	2	3	4	5
Rarely	Occasionally	Sometimes	Often	Very often

18. Were staff members helping residents move about the facility, with or without canes, walkers, splints, wheelchairs, or other assistive devices?

1	2	3	4	5
Rarely	*Occasionally*	*Sometimes*	*Often*	*Very often*

19. Were rehabilitation therapists actively working with residents to improve or restore function? (You may have to look at name badges or ask staff members to identify therapists. This question may not apply to assisted living or residential care facilities.)

1	2	3	4	5
Rarely	*Occasionally*	*Sometimes*	*Often*	*Very often*

20. Did staff members communicate with confused residents (such as residents with Alzheimer's disease) through talk, smiles, touch, etc.? (This question may not apply to assisted living or residential care facilities.)

1	2	3	4	5
Rarely	*Occasionally*	*Sometimes*	*Often*	*Very often*

21. Did confused residents have an adequate, safe place to wander indoors? (You may need to ask staff to answer this question. This question may not apply to assisted living or residential care facilities.)

1	2	3	4	5
None	Very little	Some	Enough	More than enough

22. Did confused residents have an adequate, safe place to wander outdoors? (This space should be limited so residents will not wander into unsafe areas. You may need to ask staff to answer this question. This question may not apply to assisted living or residential care facilities.)

1	2	3	4	5
None	Very little	Some	Enough	More than enough

23. Did confused residents have easy access to this outdoor space? (In some facilities, residents can only go outdoors when accompanied by a staff member, which limits the time they can spend outdoors. You may need to ask staff to answer this question. This question may not apply to assisted living or residential care facilities.)

1	2	3	4	5
No access	Very little	Some	Easy access	Very easy access

24. Did the other residents have an adequate, safe space to wander outdoors? (Some residents prefer to spend many hours outdoors, and they should be able to do so if they wish. You may need to ask staff to answer this question.)

1	2	3	4	5
None	Very little	Some	Enough	More than enough

25. Did the other residents have easy access to this outdoor space? (You may need to ask staff to answer this question.)

1	2	3	4	5
No access	Very little	Some	Easy access	Very easy access

26. Were odors of urine or feces noticeable in the facility? (These odors should not be pervasive. If they are, do not consider moving into this nursing home. A strong odor of urine or feces indicates major problems with quality of care.)

1	2	3	4	5
Constantly	Too often	Often	Occasionally	Rarely

27. Were other unpleasant odors noticeable in the facility? (When residents' personal hygiene is poor, other unpleasant odors become apparent. This should not be the case.)

1	2	3	4	5
Constantly	Too often	Often	Occasionally	Rarely

28. Were hallways and public areas uncluttered? (Because nursing homes are busy places with lots of people living and working in them, some clutter is likely. However, it should not be hazardous to walk or wheel a wheelchair throughout the building.)

1	2	3	4	5
Very cluttered	Often cluttered	Somewhat cluttered	Neat	Very neat

29. Were resident rooms, hallways, public areas, and common areas clean? (They should be free from dust, mold, mildew, stains on the floors or walls, etc.)

1	2	3	4	5
Dirty	Somewhat dirty	More or less clean	Clean	Very clean

30. Were buildings, grounds, and furniture in good condition?

1	2	3	4	5
Very poor condition	Poor condition	Fairly good condition	Good condition	Very good condition

31. Were the hallways well lighted?

1	2	3	4	5
Heavily shadowed	Poorly lighted	Some light but not enough	Well lighted	Exceptionally well lighted

32. Were the public and common areas well lighted?

1	2	3	4	5
Heavily shadowed	Poorly lighted	Some light but not enough	Well lighted	Exceptionally well lighted

The New Nursing Homes © 2001 by Marilyn Rantz, RN, PhD; et al.

33. Were resident rooms well lighted?

1	2	3	4	5
Heavily shadowed	*Poorly lighted*	*Some light but not enough*	*Well lighted*	*Exceptionally well lighted*

34. Was the environment free from loud or disturbing noises?

1	2	3	4	5
Very noisy	*Often noisy*	*Some noise*	*Little noise*	*Not noisy*

35. Did the facility seem calm?

1	2	3	4	5
Very chaotic	*Quite chaotic*	*Some chaos*	*Quite calm*	*Very calm*

36. Was there a pleasant atmosphere or feeling about the facility?

1	2	3	4	5
Very unpleasant	*Somewhat unpleasant*	*More or less pleasant*	*Quite pleasant*	*Very pleasant*

37. Were residents' rooms personalized with furniture, pictures, and other items from their past? (It is important that residents have some personal items to help them feel at home.)

1	2	3	4	5
Most were not	*A few were*	*Some were*	*Many were*	*Most were*

38. Were plants (live or artificial) and pets (dogs, cats, birds, etc.) in resident rooms?

1	2	3	4	5
Rarely	*Occasionally*	*Sometimes*	*Often*	*Very often*

39. Were plants (live or artificial) and pets (dogs, cats, birds, etc.) in public areas?

1	2	3	4	5
Rarely	*Occasionally*	*Sometimes*	*Often*	*Very often*

40. If plants and/or pets were observed, did they seem in good condition?

1	2	3	4	5
Very poor condition	Poor condition	Fairly good condition	Good condition	Very good condition

41. Did the facility look and feel like a home?

1	2	3	4	5
Not at all homelike	Somewhat	More or less	Quite	Very homelike

42. Were visitors (family members, volunteers, community members, etc.) visible in the facility?

1	2	3	4	5
Rarely	Occasionally	Sometimes	Often	Very often

Interviewing
the Staff

If, after visiting a nursing home or assisted living facility, you are interested in learning more, ask to interview an admissions staff member. You may have to make an appointment for this interview.

On the following pages, you'll find detailed interview questions about cost of care, payment options, staff workload, continuity of management and staff, safety information, and more. Each question includes the answer you're likely to hear if the facility is doing a good job. Note that some questions may not apply to assisted living facilities.

The actual questionnaire, which appears on pages 70 through 83, includes space for taking notes. Copy this questionnaire and take it with you each time you visit a facility. Note that many of the issues covered here—such as payment options and helping residents transition to nursing home life—are covered in greater detail in chapters 5 and 6.

Cost

- *Does this nursing home accept Medicare or Medicaid payment? (This question may not be applicable.)*

For many people, Medicare and Medicaid are important sources of payment for nursing home care. Some nursing homes accept Medicare for short stays. Find this out up front. If you are planning a long or permanent stay and are likely to use Medicaid, then you need to find a facility that accepts Medicaid. In most cases, long-term residents pay for nursing home care until their private funds are depleted, then they apply for Medicaid. It is important to discuss the Medicaid application process with the admissions staff prior to admission and before private funds run out, so payment arrangements can be made in a timely fashion.

Assisted living facilities do not participate in Medicare and generally do not participate in Medicaid.

- *What is the basic weekly and monthly charge?*

Charges begin at about $100 per day and can go much higher, depending on the services included. Prices vary from state to state, depending on Medicaid payment rates. Private pay rates vary widely, depending upon services and the type of room.

- *What items are not covered in the basic charge?*

  Be sure to ask about these potentially "hidden" charges so you can plan for the costs. Frequently there are additional charges for things like:

medications	beauty/barber shop
wheelchair	dietary supplements
transportation	incontinence supplies
dentist	

- *Before the resident receives any service not covered by insurance, such as dental care, will the family be notified?*

  The family should be notified in advance of services that will need to be paid for.

- *Is an advanced payment required? If so, will it be returned if the resident leaves the facility?*

  Sometimes facilities will require one or two months' payment in advance. All or part of this should be returned if the resident leaves early.

Building and rooms

- *Can residents bring furniture from their home?*

  Residents should be allowed—and encouraged—to bring chairs, a dresser, or other pieces of furniture, as well as pictures and other personal items that make a room more homelike.

- *Can residents bring a pet?*

  Some facilities encourage residents to bring a family pet, if the pet is sociable and if the resident is able to tend to it. At some places, the staff helps out with pet care.

- *Can pets visit?*

  Pet visitation should be encouraged. Be sure the pet is clean, and be mindful of proper disposal of animal waste. Also remember that other residents or family members may not enjoy animals.

- *Is there adequate storage space for personal items, both in the room and in a general storage area?*

  There should be room to store off-season clothing, small seasonal decorations, and other items. The resident's family may want to store some of his or her belongings at home. Valuable items should always be stored at home.

- *If this is a multistory building, are there adequate elevators to transport residents?*

  There should be enough elevators for residents to easily get from place to place. Be sure to see for yourself that the elevators are adequate.

- *Is there outdoor space for residents to enjoy?*

  Residents should be able to spend time outdoors. For those who may wander, there should be a safe outdoor space designed to prevent them from leaving the grounds.

- *How are smokers' and nonsmokers' wishes addressed?*

  There should be a separate, well-ventilated area where residents may safely smoke without polluting the air for others. Staff smoking areas should not be at a public entrance.

- *How does the staff know if residents leave the building?*

  Some residents should not leave the building without supervision. It is important that doors have alarms so the staff knows when residents leave. Some facilities use electronic devices that sound an alarm when residents pass through the doorway.

- *Does the building have a sprinkler system in case of fire?*

  It should have.

- *If there is a fire, how will the staff make sure the residents are safe?*

  The staff should have a detailed plan and be able to explain it.

Staff

- *How long have the last two administrators worked here?*

  Consistent leadership tends to improve care. A facility with a stable administration is more likely to deliver better services than one with constant turnover. Administrators should stay several years.

- *How long have the last two directors of nursing worked here?*

  A director of nursing who stays with a facility for several years is likely to have staff and care delivery systems in place. Turnover in this position could indicate problems in delivery of care.

- *How long has the current owner of the facility owned and operated it?*

Facilities with stable, long-term ownership are more likely to have the staff and care delivery systems in place than those where ownership changes frequently.

- *Are there licensed nurses on all three shifts (day, evening, and night)? (This question may not be applicable.)*

There should be licensed nurses on all three shifts. Licensed practical nurses (LPNs) have nine to twelve months of education and training beyond high school. Their job is to evaluate resident needs and see that each resident gets the care that he or she requires. One national resident advocacy organization recommends LPN-to-patient ratios of 1:15 on days, 1:25 on evenings, and 1:35 on nights. Staffing will vary depending upon the residents in the nursing home and the kind of care they need.

- *Are the same registered nurses responsible for the same residents each day? (This question may not be applicable.)*

The same registered nurses (RNs) should care for the same residents. RNs have two to four years of college education. They are responsible for knowing each resident's medical condition and recognizing when there are changes that need attention. If they care for the same residents each day, they will get to know them well enough to notice significant physical or emotional changes.

- *How many residents does each nursing assistant care for on each shift? (This question may not be applicable.)*

Nursing assistants provide most of the direct care, so there ought to be enough assistants to help residents eat, dress, bathe, and go to the toilet. A national resident advocacy organization recommends direct caregiver ratios of 1:5 residents on days, 1:10 on evenings, and 1:15 on nights. Staffing will vary depending on recruitment, staffing policies at the facility, and the kind of care that residents need.

• *Do residents have the same nursing assistants caring for them day in and day out?*

They should have. When nursing assistants are assigned to the same residents each shift, they can get to know their residents well, and this often improves the quality of care.

• *Do residents have the same housekeeper cleaning their room each time?*

Residents get to know the housecleaning staff, and having the same housekeeper is reassuring. Housekeepers often become a source of social support.

• *Does this facility use staff from a temporary employment agency?*

Because temporary workers do not know the individual residents or their special needs, overreliance on temporary staff can cause problems.Occasional backup from an agency may be necessary, especially in some urban areas where businesses must compete for quality staff members. However, something is wrong if a nursing home routinely relies on temporary workers for regular staffing.

- *What are nursing assistants, housekeepers, and dietary staff paid? How does this compare to wages paid by other nursing homes in the community?*

  Employee wages should be comparable to those at other nursing homes in the community. Workers who are fairly compensated are more likely to stay with their employers, and this often results in higher quality of care. As you visit different nursing homes, you'll get a better idea of how their wages compare.

- *Is there a registered dietitian available? (This question may not be applicable.)*

  There should be a registered dietitian available.

- *Are physical therapy, speech therapy, and occupational therapy available? (This question may not be applicable.)*

  There should be rehabilitation therapists available.

Transition to facility life

- *How does the staff help new residents adjust to the facility?*

  Staff members should be able to explain how they help new residents adjust. They might use a welcome banner, new residents' teas, social service visitation, activity staff visits, and other efforts to involve new residents in nursing home life.

- *How do current residents help new residents adjust to the facility?*

  They may have a resident visitation, a welcome committee, or other ways to greet new residents.

- *What are typical problems that new residents have when they come to this facility? How does the staff help them handle these problems?*

  The staff should be able to explain common problems that concern new residents and how they can help.

- *How are residents matched as roommates? (This question may not be applicable.)*

  The staff should try to match interests, healthcare needs, ability to get along, and other characteristics. Nursing homes typically have two beds per room; most assisted living facilities have private rooms.

- *What happens if roommates do not get along? (This question may not be applicable.)*

  Residents should have some recourse if they cannot get along with their roommate. The staff may suggest another roommate or unit, or they might arrange a meeting between the roommates and a social worker to try to resolve the conflict.

- *Do residents refer to the nursing home as "their home now"?*

  Ideally, as residents adjust, they tend to refer to the nursing home as their home.

- *Are there other residents here who might be interested in socializing?*

  The staff should be aware of other residents who may be a good social match for you or your loved one.

Opportunities for resident and family input

- *Is there a family advisory or support group?*

  There should be. Family groups can help residents and their families adjust to nursing home life.

- *Do families and residents meet routinely with the administrator, director of nursing, or the other staff to discuss care and life issues?*

  You should be able to meet regularly with the staff to discuss care concerns and share ideas to make nursing home life even better.

- *Is there a resident council?*

  Most nursing homes have a resident council where residents routinely meet with the staff to discuss care and nursing home life.

- *Is there a family council?*

  Many homes have family councils so families can routinely advise the staff about care and quality of life issues to improve service.

Care issues

- *What do residents usually say about the food?*

  The staff should know if residents like the food in general, or if they usually like some meals more than others.

- *What happens if a resident does not want to eat a particular meal?*

  Residents should be given alternative choices. Ask what substitutions are available to residents today.

- *Are residents able to request special food items?*

  Residents should be able to make special requests. Families should be encouraged to bring in special foods that their family member particularly wants.

- *Can I taste the food and observe a meal?*

  The staff should let you taste a meal prepared for the residents. Watch a meal being served. It should look and smell appetizing.

- *Is there a program to help residents regain their physical abilities?*

  There should be an organized program. In most homes this program is part of the basic daily care rate, but you should ask just to be sure. If there is a separate charge, ask what residents gain from the program and how much it costs.

- *Are residents assisted to the bathroom when they ask?*

  They should be.

- *Are toilets conveniently located for resident use?*

  They should be.

- *Are there grab bars and other safety devices in resident bathrooms?*

  There should be.

- *How does the staff help residents maintain privacy and dignity when they are given baths, toileting assistance, and other care?*

Staff members should tell you how important it is for residents to maintain privacy and dignity. They should have an orientation program to teach new staff how to preserve a residents' dignity when providing care. When you tour the facility, you should not see residents exposed inappropriately while they are given care.

- *How long do residents typically wait until their light is answered? (May not be applicable.)*

Although staff members cannot always respond immediately, residents should not have to wait fifteen minutes or longer for help. Make a point of watching when you tour the facility to see if there are lots of call lights on and if staff are responding to them.

- *What activities are available?*

There should be a variety of activities to interest a variety of people. Many nursing homes offer craft groups; music groups; shopping trips; exercise groups; small discussion groups; games like bingo and bunko; and field trips to fairs, festivals, and other community events. In addition, individual activities, such as reading or playing cards, should be encouraged. There should also be activities for residents with reduced mental capacity.

- *How frequently are activities offered?*

Activities should be offered frequently so residents can socialize, explore new interests, and occupy their time. Occasional evening and weekend activities should supplement traditional mid-morning and mid-afternoon events.

- *Are religious services conducted for the residents? How often?*

  Services should address the needs of people with different religions, and should be frequent enough to meet residents' interests. Ask about services that will meet your needs or the needs of your loved one.

- *Can residents leave the nursing home for an outing or other leisure activity?*

  There should be opportunities for an occasional outing. Families should be encouraged to take their loved one out to a favorite restaurant, a wedding, or family celebrations.

- *Do residents have the freedom to say no when they don't want something or would prefer not to do something?*

  Sometimes residents do not want certain medical treatments, or they prefer not to participate in some activities. They should have the right to say no. Treatment decisions should be discussed with the resident's doctor, family, and staff so everyone understands what the resident wants.

- *How does the staff work to avoid using physical restraints?*

  There should be an organized effort to help staff members find ways of dealing with difficult behaviors without the use of physical restraints. When you tour the nursing home, you should not see residents tied to chairs or beds. The staff should be managing behavior so physical restraints are rarely, if ever, used. Restraints do not prevent falls and can cause harm by reducing walking and other body motions that people need to maintain strength.

Interviewing the Staff

Restraints can cause additional problems like skin breakdown, strangulation, increased incontinence, and depression.

- *How does the staff avoid the use of siderails?*

As with restraints, staff members should assess why siderails are used. Siderails can be very dangerous and do not protect residents from falling out of bed. In fact, if a resident attempts to get out of bed and falls over the siderail, the risk of serious injury is high. Siderails should not be used uniformly for all residents. When they are used, the decision to do so should be carefully considered.

- *How does the staff help residents who are depressed?*

Staff members should be able to describe a number of techniques, such as talking frequently with the residents, trying to involve them in activities, getting a psychological evaluation, and more.

- *Who is the ombudsman for this facility? Does the ombudsman visit regularly? (May not be applicable.)*

Nursing homes have an ombudsman, a consumer advocate who is a part of the official state ombudsman program. Ombudsmen investigate and attempt to resolve concerns raised by nursing home residents, their families, or their friends. The staff should be able to tell you who the ombudsman is and when he or she usually comes to the nursing home to see residents.

Alzheimer's care

- *Are there special services and activities for residents with Alzheimer's disease?*

  Because these residents have special needs, special services should be available. For example, a quiet environment can minimize confusion and reduce agitated behavior. Special activities can help occupy residents and minimize wandering. Some facilities will have a special unit to care for Alzheimer's patients.

- *Is the staff specially trained to care for Alzheimer's patients?*

  It should be. Staff members should be taught about the special needs of residents with Alzheimer's disease.

- *Are doors secured or fitted with alarms so residents with Alzheimer's cannot wander outside without a staff member?*

  If doors lead out of the building or to other areas in the facility, they should be secure. Many special units are designed so residents have a safe, limited space to wander both indoors and outdoors. Some units are designed so when residents go outside, the staff can see them at all times. In this case, the doors do not need alarms.

- *Do residents on the special unit have a safe space to enjoy outdoors?*

  They should. The space should be inviting, and it should provide shade in warm weather and protection from colder weather. Residents must not be able to wander into other areas where they might be harmed.

The Staff Questions

Facility _____ Date _____ Time _____

Cost

1. Does this nursing home accept Medicare or Medicaid payment? (May not apply.)

2. What is the basic weekly and monthly charge?

3. What items are not covered in the basic charge?

   ___ Medications   ___ Dentist   ___ Incontinence supplies
   ___ Wheelchair   ___ Beauty/barber shop   ___ Other: _____
   ___ Transportation   ___ Dietary supplements

The New Nursing Homes © 2001 by Marilyn Rantz, RN, PhD; et al.

4. Before the resident receives any service not covered by insurance, such as dental care, will the family be notified?

5. Is an advanced payment required? If so, will it be returned if the resident leaves the facility?

Building and rooms

6. Can residents bring furniture from their home?

7. Can residents bring a pet?

8. Can pets visit?

9. Is there adequate storage space for personal items, both in the room and in a general storage area?

10. If this is a multistory building, are there adequate elevators to transport residents?

11. Is there outdoor space for residents to enjoy?

12. How are smokers' and nonsmokers' wishes addressed?

13. How does the staff know if residents leave the building?

14. Does the building have a sprinkler system in case of fire?

15. If there is a fire, how will the staff make sure the residents are safe?

Staff

16. How long have the last two administrators worked here?

17. How long have the last two directors of nursing worked here?

18. How long has the current owner of the facility owned and operated it?

19. Are there licensed nurses on all three shifts (day, evening, and night)? (May not apply.)

20. Are the same registered nurses responsible for the same residents each day? (May not apply.)

21. How many residents does each nursing assistant care for on each shift? (May not apply.)

22. Do residents have the same nursing assistants caring for them day in and day out?

23. Do residents have the same housekeeper cleaning their room each time?

24. Does this facility use staff from a temporary employment agency?

25. What are nursing assistants, housekeepers, and dietary staff paid? How does this compare to wages paid by other nursing homes in the community?

26. Is there a registered dietitian available? (May not apply.)

27. Are physical therapy, speech therapy, and occupational therapy available? (May not apply.)

Transition to facility life

28. How does the staff help new residents adjust to the facility?

29. How do current residents help new residents adjust to the facility?

30. What are typical problems that new residents have when they come to this facility? How does the staff help them handle these problems?

31. How are residents matched as roommates? (May not apply.)

32. What happens if roommates do not get along? (May not apply.)

33. Do residents refer to the nursing home as "their home now"?

34. Are there other residents here who might be interested in socializing?

Opportunities for resident and family input

35. Is there a family advisory or support group?

36. Do families and residents meet routinely with the administrator, director of nursing, or the other staff to discuss care and life issues?

37. Is there a resident council?

38. Is there a family council?

Care issues

39. What do residents usually say about the food?

40. What happens if a resident does not want to eat a particular meal?

41. Are residents able to request special food items?

42. Can I taste the food and observe a meal?

43. Is there a program to help residents regain their physical abilities?

44. Are residents assisted to the bathroom when they ask?

45. Are toilets conveniently located for resident use?

46. Are there grab bars and other safety devices in resident bathrooms?

47. How does the staff help residents maintain privacy and dignity when they are given baths, toileting assistance, and other care?

48. How long do residents typically wait until their light is answered? (May not apply.)

49. What activities are available?

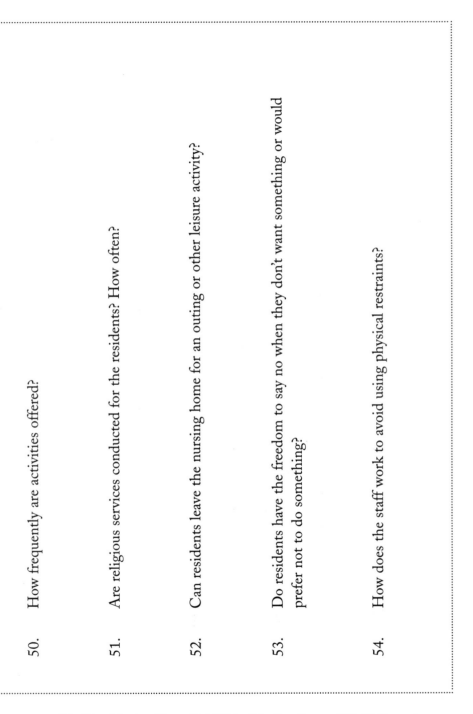

50. How frequently are activities offered?

51. Are religious services conducted for the residents? How often?

52. Can residents leave the nursing home for an outing or other leisure activity?

53. Do residents have the freedom to say no when they don't want something or would prefer not to do something?

54. How does the staff work to avoid using physical restraints?

55. How does the staff avoid the use of siderails?

56. How does the staff help residents who are depressed?

57. Who is the ombudsman for this facility? Does the ombudsman visit regularly? (May not apply.)

Alzheimer's care

58. Are there special services and activities for residents with Alzheimer's disease?

59. Is the staff specially trained to care for Alzheimer's patients?

60. Are doors secured or fitted with alarms so residents cannot wander outside without a staff member?

61. Do residents on the special unit have a safe space to enjoy outdoors?

Interviewing
Families

If, after touring a facility and interviewing staff members, you think you've found a good fit for yourself or your loved one, we recommend interviewing people who have family members living there. Strike up conversations with other visitors as you tour the facility. Tell them what you are considering, and ask if they'd be willing to talk about their own experiences.

This chapter contains important questions to help you elicit different impressions of a facility's staff and policies. As in chapter 3, we provide a sample of a "good" answer for each question. Note that some questions may not apply to assisted living facilities.

You'll find the actual questionnaire on pages 90 through 95; make as many copies as you need, and use a new copy for each interview. Feel free to ask your own questions as well.

- *Does your loved one seem to enjoy certain parts of the day (events, mealtimes, etc.), every day?*

  The resident should. Ask family members for examples.

- *Do you think your loved one is treated with respect and courtesy?*

  All residents should be. Ask for examples.

- *Are residents encouraged to be as independent as possible?*

  They should be, though abilities differ among residents.

- *How often do you visit?*

  Responses will vary. Try to get a sense of whether people feel they must visit to make sure the staff is taking care of their loved one. Also, try to learn whether they're afraid to leave their family member alone for some reason.

- *Is the staff positive toward your visits?*

  It should be. If not, ask why the family thinks this is so.

- *Is there a call-light system that your loved one can use? Are staff members responsive to the lights and other requests for care? (May not be applicable.)*

  Although a reliable call system should be installed in every nursing home, the staff cannot respond to each request immediately, just as families cannot do so in day-to-day living. However, residents should not have to wait fifteen minutes or longer every time they request help, especially if they need help with the toilet. The staff should be responsive enough to see that needs are met in a timely fashion. (Note that call lights in assisted living facilities are typically for emergency use only.)

- *Do the same staff members regularly care for your loved one?*
Staff continuity helps ensure better care.

- *Do staff members seem to know your loved one as a person? Are they able to talk to your loved one about details of his or her life?*
The staff should know the residents well, and they should be receptive to residents who try to share details of their lives.

- *Does the staff know what kind of care your loved one needs?*
It should.

- *Do you think the staff takes proper care of your loved one?*
Although few family members are experts in nursing home care, observation and intuition should tell them that their loved one is well cared for.

- *Has your loved one ever complained of not being treated well?*
If so, try to determine the circumstances. Did the staff seem to be deliberately mistreating the resident?

- *Do you think the staff listens to you?*
Families should feel that staff members listen, and they should be able to give you an example or two to support this.

- *Does your loved one feel like this is home now?*

  He or she should, but remember that this can take time. Find out how long this person has been a resident.

- *Do staff members encourage residents to remain continent?*

  They should. Staff members should take residents to the bathroom when they ask to go. Families should never hear the staff say, "You have a diaper on, so it is okay to just go ahead and go!"

- *Are residents and families involved in care planning? (May not be applicable.)*

  The staff should ask family members for input, then incorporate their suggestions into a written care plan. Care-plan meetings are scheduled to review and discuss the care that each resident needs and that the staff will provide. Residents and family members should be invited and encouraged to participate in routine care-plan meetings—and care planning in general.

- *Does the staff follow up on issues raised in care-plan meetings? (May not be applicable.)*

  Family members should be able to offer an example or two of how the staff followed through on such issues.

- *Is your loved one fearful of complaining?*

  Residents should be able to state reasonable complaints without fear. Fearfulness is common among people who are confused or mentally ill, but residents with these problems should not be excessively fearful.

- *If you complain, are your complaints addressed?*

  Try to get a sense of the family member's complaint, how it was broached, and how the staff responded.

- *Have you been concerned about personal items being lost or misplaced?*

  This happens, but it should not be common. (Tip: Because personal items can be difficult to keep track of, make sure they are clearly marked so staff members know which belongings go with which resident. Expensive items, such as heirloom jewelry, should be kept at home. Provide costume jewelry for a loved one to wear—if it is misplaced, you will not have lost a family keepsake.)

- *If your loved one is injured or becomes ill, does the staff contact you quickly?*

  It should.

- *Does your loved one feel safe and secure in this facility?*

  He or she should.

- *Have you ever been concerned about your loved one's safety?*

  Although nursing homes are not risk-free, listen for excessive concern. Ask what the family knows about security precautions at the nursing home and their effectiveness.

- *Knowing what you know now, if you had to choose a nursing home today, would you still select this one?*

  If the family is satisfied with the care and services, they would.

Questions for Family Members

Facility _____

Name _____ Date _____ Time _____

1. Does your loved one seem to enjoy certain parts of the day (events, mealtimes, etc.), every day?

2. Do you think your loved one is treated with respect and courtesy?

3. Are residents encouraged to be as independent as possible?

4. How often do you visit?

5. Is the staff positive toward your visits?

6. Is there a call-light system that your loved one can use? Are staff members responsive to the lights and other requests for care? (May not apply.)

7. Do the same staff members regularly care for your loved one?

8. Do staff members seem to know your loved one? As a person? Are they able to talk to your loved one about details of his or her life?

9. Does the staff know what kind of care your loved one needs?

10. Do you think the staff takes proper care of your loved one?

11. Has your loved one ever complained of not being treated well?

12. Do you think the staff listens to you?

13. Does your loved one feel like this is home now?

14. Do staff members encourage residents to remain continent?

15. Are residents and families involved in care planning? (May not apply.)

16. Does the staff follow up on issues raised in care-plan meetings? (May not apply.)

17. Is your loved one fearful of complaining?

18. If you complain, are your complaints addressed?

19. Have you been concerned about personal items being lost or misplaced?

20. If your loved one is injured or becomes ill, does the staff contact you quickly?

21. Does your loved one feel safe and secure in this facility?

22. Have you ever been concerned about your loved one's safety?

23. Knowing what you know now, if you had to choose a nursing home today, would you still select this one?

5

Who Will Pay?

The cost of nursing home care can run from $40,000 to $60,000 a year—a staggering amount for most people. But don't lose heart. Financing alternatives do exist. Your four basic options are Medicaid, Medicare, long-term care insurance, and personal funds. In the following pages, we describe these options in broad terms. However, the rules and regulations are constantly changing, and they vary from state to state, so you'll need to ask your nursing home social worker to help you sort through the details.

Medicaid

THE VAST MAJORITY of nursing homes participate in the Medicaid program, a state-sponsored welfare program that helps many people who cannot afford to pay for medical care. In fact, Medicaid pays 60 percent of all nursing home bills nationwide. In a few states, Medicaid may also pay for other long-term care options, including assisted living or residential care, board-and-care homes, and some community-based services.

If you think you might use Medicaid to pay for nursing home care—whether now or in the future—you must:

1. Be sure the nursing home you choose is Medicaid certified.

2. Check with the nursing home staff to be certain the resident needs the kind of care that the nursing home delivers. (Medicaid requires preadmission screenings to make sure residents need the kind of care they'll be getting.)

3. Find out if the resident will qualify for Medicaid. (The nursing home social worker will help you through the process and answer any questions you may have.)

To qualify for Medicaid, most people are required to contribute a substantial amount of their income—typically a social security check—before the state will pick up the balance. Widowed and unmarried people must "spend down" their assets to about $2,000 before coverage starts. This means they must sell their home unless they can establish that they will probably return to it. For individuals who have a spouse living at home, many assets, including the residence and some income, are exempt. So, a resident's spouse could keep the home, car, clothing, and up to $80,000 in other assets such as stocks, bonds, pension income, savings, and bank accounts, although this can vary widely by state.

Some attorneys specialize in arranging assets in a way that works to a person's advantage *and* lets him or her qualify for Medicaid. If you or your loved one are interested in arranging your assets, find an attorney who specializes in estate planning. Remember, laws vary from state to state. Penalties for divesting assets in an attempt to qualify for Medicaid are high, and you or your loved one could be disqualified from receiving any future Medicaid assistance. Always consult an attorney when handling assets, and be sure you know the laws in your state.

Mr. and Mrs. Brown

Mr. Brown has experienced declining health for several years, having been diagnosed with dementia and other chronic illnesses. His wife of fifty years had been caring for him, but her own health was challenged by her daily and nightly caregiving responsibilities—until their physician finally recommended nursing home care for Mr. Brown.

The admissions staff at the nursing home, along with the county aging service that approves Medicaid applications, helped Mrs. Brown arrange payment for her husband's nursing home care. She retained ownership of their home, car, personal effects, and a portion of their life savings. Mr. Brown's portion has purchased prepaid burial services and his initial care in the nursing home. When these funds are gone, Medicaid will take over. Mrs. Brown is relieved—her husband now has twenty-four-hour care, and her home is still her home.

Medicare

MEDICARE, A FEDERAL insurance program, will sometimes cover short-term stays in a nursing home. Although most people qualify for Medicare coverage at age sixty-five, not all nursing homes are Medicare certified. To receive Medicare payment, a nursing home must complete a special certification process. (Note that a facility's Medicare certification is not a guarantee of quality.)

Medicare will cover nursing home care only under certain conditions. Typically, coverage follows hospitalization. If the resident qualifies, Medicare will pay the nursing home bill for the first twenty days. After that, a copayment of about $96 per day is required. (Many supplemental Medicare insurance policies will pay for all or most of this copayment.) The maximum number of days covered is usually one hundred. When coverage runs out, the resident must switch to Medicaid or private payment, according to his or her financial situation.

As a general rule, if you anticipate a short nursing home stay after a hospitalization, you should look for a Medicare-certified nursing home. If you anticipate a long-term or permanent stay, then Medicare certification is not an important criterion.

Medicare benefits are extremely complicated, and you will need help from the nursing home billing staff to determine exactly what will be paid for.

Long-term care insurance

LONG-TERM CARE INSURANCE may pay for some or all of a resident's nursing home care, depending upon the coverage purchased. Typically, there are limits on the daily payments and the duration of coverage. (For example, a policy might pay

Mrs. Grant

Mrs. Grant fell in her home and fractured her right hip. She was hospitalized, and the hip was surgically repaired. After a few days, her physician suggested that a short stay in a nursing home would help her finish rehabilitation so she could return home.

Mrs. Grant had Medicare coverage and a supplemental insurance policy. Her son and daughter-in-law located a good nursing home in their community—it scored well on the walk-through, and they were satisfied with the responses they received during the staff and family interviews. In addition, the home was certified to accept Medicare payment. Mrs. Grant received care and rehabilitation services for four weeks, then returned home. Most charges were paid by Medicare and her supplemental insurance. Some additional charges—beauty shop and podiatry—had to be paid by Mrs. Grant.

$120 per day for three years.) Some long-term care insurance will cover home care services, but, again, limitations will vary from policy to policy.

For most people, the premiums for long-term care insurance are only affordable if they bought their policy in their fifties or sixties. Generally, people in their seventies can only buy insurance if they have lots of money. Even then, they should be wary of any company that is willing to sell them a policy at their age.

If you choose to buy long-term care insurance, do your homework. Make sure the company is reputable and financially sound. Many people have been victimized by dishonest companies, and some states are starting to regulate vigorously the sale of these policies. You might want to check with your local agency on aging, which likely provides assistance, advice, and advocacy for older adults seeking insurance.

In general, long-term care insurance is appropriate for people who have significant assets they want to protect. Typical policies have a three- to six-month waiting period before they begin to pay for nursing home care. If the resident exhausts all his or her assets during this period, he or she would probably qualify for Medicaid. In this case, the insurance premiums would be a waste of money.

Ms. Lewis

Ms. Lewis is a forty-five-year-old woman who has had an active career in publishing. During the past five years she has developed severe multiple sclerosis. She needs help in meeting all her physical needs. Her mother and father first helped her stay at her own home. Then she stayed with them for a year with the help of in-home health services. As Ms. Lewis continued to need more care, she and her family decided to look for a good nursing home. They found one in a small town about forty miles from where Ms. Lewis used to work. The home accepts only private-pay residents, so Ms. Lewis and her parents are planning to pay for the services out of her investment savings and, if necessary, out of their own investments. They have more than enough assets to cover the cost of care for many years to come.

Personal funds

IF YOU OR YOUR loved one are fortunate enough to have the resources to pay for an extended or permanent stay in a nursing home, you will have your pick of facilities, services, and accommodations.

Churches, fraternal organizations, and some for-profit companies will sometimes sponsor upscale facilities that cater to private-pay residents. There are relatively few of these facilities, but they tend to provide more care (at a higher cost) since they have fewer financial constraints.

Remember, if the resident outlives his or her assets, and the nursing home is not Medicaid certified, then the resident will have to move to a Medicaid-certified facility.

How to survive the paperwork

BEFORE RECEIVING MEDICAID or other public assistance, applicants must show that they qualify. They will be asked to share details about life insurance policies and beneficiaries, income tax records, retirement benefits, and other financial information. They may also need to submit a physician-verified document describing their care needs. The amount of paperwork involved can be intimidating, so it's best to ask upfront for a complete list of the documents required.

Also, be sure the nursing home has a copy of the resident's living will and durable power of attorney for healthcare. If these don't exist, it's best to create them so the resident's wishes will be carried out in the event of future illness or injury.

6 Making It Work

Once you have found a high-quality nursing home and gone through the admissions process, you and your entire family will have a period of adjustment. During this time, you will need to shift your attention to making nursing home life the best it can be.

From the start, it's important to get involved with activities and care planning. You must also focus on making the staff your ally, communicating your expectations clearly, and advocating for the best care possible.

What does this move mean?

WHEN AN INDIVIDUAL moves into a nursing home, it takes time for the new resident and his or her family to grieve for what has been lost and to adjust to nursing home life. Family members may have to assume new roles. They might feel guilt and remorse, thinking they should have somehow prevented the need for nursing home care. Residents and family members may suddenly have an acute awareness of their own mortality.

Some nursing home residents make the move because they do not want to burden family members. In other cases, the family decides or forces a decision. Regardless, leaving one's own residence can be a painful and difficult event that, to some, signifies a loss of independence. Some older adults feel that the move just shows they have "lived too long."

As upsetting as this adjustment period may be, it's normal for both the resident and the family to feel any number of emotions during this time. In fact, even nursing home workers must adjust to the move as they get to know the new resident and family and learn how best to meet their needs.

The resident adjusts

MANY PEOPLE FIND themselves needing nursing home care when they least expect it. Often, the move follows a hospitalization, when an individual feels especially unprepared to undertake such a life event. If you are moving into a nursing home, allow your family and hospital staff to help you during this time, but remember, the decisions are yours to make.

You may feel many things before and during your relocation to the nursing home. Anger, fear, frustration, and loneliness are common—as are a sense of relief and a feeling of safety. Allow yourself to feel your emotions, but recognize that your loved ones are working through emotions of their own. Give yourself some time to adjust, and try to be patient with yourself and others.

Be willing to participate in the activities at the nursing home; you can always decide later not to attend. And make sure your room is decorated with your own possessions. Have your family or friends bring in your favorite quilt, some favorite pictures, and other things you love.

Let staff members know your preferences. For example, tell them when you prefer to go to bed at night and if you prefer to have a bath in the morning or the evening. Many facilities will try very hard to plan your care to meet your preferences.

Try to spend at least some part of every day doing something you would have done at home. For example, read, pray, pet the facility cat, or watch your favorite television programs. This will help to normalize your days, easing your adjustment to nursing home life.

> "It was hard for me to make this move, but this is home now and I like it. I have my own room. I could never share a room with someone, so I am lucky to have my own room. The staff helps me and the food is good."

The family adjusts

MOST PEOPLE NEVER think that their loved ones, no matter how old or frail, will ever have to enter a nursing home. When the need for nursing home care becomes apparent, family members hate that they can't do more, be more. In many cases, the caregiver simply can no longer continue the fight alone. Eventually, anyone can run out of energy.

If your loved one has entered a nursing home, expect to feel some grief. You may feel you've let your loved one down. In addition, your family house, the scene of your childhood, may be gone now, and things will never be the same.

As you help your loved one make the transition, it is important to take care of yourself, too. If you have been the primary caregiver until now, you may be very tired. Feelings may be close to the surface. Just knowing that this is normal will help you cope.

If your family member has entered the nursing home against his or her will, you may be made to feel guilty for forcing the move. Your loved one may show his or her anger by placing unreasonable demands on your time and attention. It's important to try to meet your family member's needs without placing yourself in an impossibly demanding situation. So, plan a reasonable visiting schedule and stick to it. If you have siblings, try to alternate visits so your loved one has plenty of company. This may be the time to ask for help from your friends as well.

Visits needn't be long. Just dropping in at different times on different days may well satisfy your resident and allow you to see that things are going fine.

With your loved one in a nursing home, you now have help. You can rest, renew relationships, and try to envision the future. Your family member will be safe when you're not there. Others are there to help—to make sure your loved one has food, activities, company, and healthcare. Insulin will be given, hypoglycemia will be treated, and bingo will be played.

As for your own integration into nursing home life, you may want to consider volunteering to help with nursing home activities, such as fundraising events or crafts or sing-alongs. As a volunteer, you will meet family members of other residents and will likely find many things you have in common, including this adjustment process. Work with staff members to help them give your family member the best possible care. Help your loved one get involved in nursing home life, make new friends, renew old interests, and be as independent as possible.

> "My husband and I decided to become volunteers. You really get to know the staff and residents well that way. And it makes us feel better knowing that we're helping the residents."

Pick up your life again. If, before the move, you had been dedicating a great deal of time and energy to helping your loved one remain independent, the new arrangement should give you much-needed time to reconnect with your family and friends. This is the time to be with other people you love. Enjoy the activities that you simply didn't have time for before. And rest. Shed the feelings of exhaustion that have become so common they feel normal to you now.

Overcoming the awkwardness of the first visits

It may seem odd, but visitors often don't know what to do when they call on someone, even a close family member, in a nursing home. It may help to bring along "props" to make everyone more comfortable and to have something to talk about. Bring family photos—large ones if eyesight is poor—or perhaps something you found at a rummage sale that reminds you of your loved one's past. If your family member is depressed or confused, conversation may be difficult, so try bringing seasonal foods, such as oranges or strawberries. Savor the fruit together, and reminisce about fruits from different seasons.

"My dad can't talk with me anymore—he has severe dementia. But he loves strawberries. I try to find the biggest ones to bring when I visit. We sit, and I talk about the kids and work, and we eat strawberries together. He seems content. It makes me feel better, even though he can't talk."

Bring along a favorite pet. Dogs, cats, and other animals really spark reactions from residents. Encourage your resident to stroke the animal. Talk about other animals from the past. Bring children along, too, as well as toys for them to play with. Some nursing homes have an area for children to play in while you visit with your family member. Talk about the things the children are doing, or broaden the conversation to other children in the family, as well as the things you and your loved one did as children. If the nursing home will lend you a VCR, bring along a favorite movie or videos of family parties, graduations, and weddings.

"We bring the kids and their toys—it makes our visits easier. Mom still gets upset at times, but my kids make her smile. They love to come here and see everyone. I make sure they have toys to keep them somewhat occupied, but before you know it they're in the activity room with other residents, the dog who lives here, and the activities staff."

One woman we know lives far from the nursing home where her father now stays. She writes him several large-type letters a week. In one short letter she mentioned that the weather had been good and the farmers were out planting corn. She went on to say, "Remember, Dad, how you always planted our corn in the straightest rows in the county?" Her father likes to get mail, and staff members enjoy reading the letters to him. His daughter includes information from his past so the staff will continue to learn about him and always have something new to talk with him about.

Visits are about being with another person. Even if a family member is not able to converse, there are other fine ways to spend time together. Try walking with the resident or wheeling about the home to visit other areas. Or, try a hand massage. People need and want to be touched, and hand massages are particularly soothing for many people. Ask other families and staff members for ideas that might make your visits more meaningful.

Warning signs to watch for

New residents may show signs of depression, including crying, unreasonable anger with oneself and others, withdrawal or refusal to become active in the home, loss of appetite and resulting weight loss, a change in sleep or activity patterns, new or increased mentions of physical illness, and repetitive questions or complaints. Allow your loved one time to adjust, but discuss the situation with the nursing home staff, especially social workers and activity directors.

When should you ask about calling in a psychiatrist or other mental health professional? If your loved one is losing weight or doesn't seem to be settling in after several weeks, it may be time to call for this additional help. The doctor might prescribe an antidepressant medication; however, this can take two to four weeks to work effectively, so it is best not to linger over the decision to call a psychiatrist.

Sometimes, moving to a nursing home causes residents to have a period of confusion, but this should pass as they adjust to the new environment.

Adjustment can best be gauged by whether a resident does some of the same things he or she did before coming to the nursing home. For example, if your loved one is an active person who has always gotten involved with others, is he or she getting to know the other residents? If your loved one has always been a quiet reader, is he or she beginning to read again? As a rule of thumb, people who were quite social before moving into a nursing home are the quickest to meet others and become involved in activities. These people may have an easier time adjusting.

How to respond to confusion

If your loved one suffers from a dementing illness, such as Alzheimer's disease, moving to a nursing home may cause an increase in confusion. Because agitated behavior will commonly occur around the same time each day, it's important for the staff to get to know your resident's schedule. Any behavior patterns you noticed at home will most likely occur in the nursing home, too. The more information you can give the staff, the better. For example, a woman who had many children or grandchildren may begin to look for kids coming home from school at 3:30 in the afternoon. A man who owned a dairy farm may well wake at 5:00 in the morning to milk the cows. Be sure staff members are aware of such behaviors so they can plan interventions to keep your loved one busy during times of confusion.

When speaking with a confused resident, we recommend using a validation and distraction technique, rather than attempting to reorient the person. For example, when a man asks to talk with his wife who has been dead for several years, ask him to tell you about her. What was she like, what did she like to do, what did she look like? While talking about his wife, the man may remember for himself that she is dead, or he may go on to another activity without becoming agitated and upset. Do not try to reorient the man by telling him that his wife died years ago and he cannot speak to her. Confronting him may well cause an agitated, angry, or bitter grief response. Discuss what she was like and move on to another topic. This is a much kinder and effective approach for dealing with confusion.

Often, nursing homes have special care units for people with Alzheimer's disease or other dementia. These units should have staff members who are specially trained to deal with confused residents. There should be a safe place to wander both indoors and outdoors, and there should be a variety of activities to help engage older adults with dementia.

The benefits of a family council

If a family council or other family group doesn't yet exist in the nursing home, help start one. Family groups serve two important functions: to help families get to know one another, and to identify problems affecting the residents.

Through a family group, you and your loved one will meet other families and residents, and you will have more to talk about as you make new friends. When families come together, they can make the nursing home even better.

Family groups can work with the staff to seek constructive and innovative solutions to any problems that arise. In fact, families often have concerns that the nursing staff, director of nursing, or administrator needs to know about—housekeeping problems, malfunctioning machinery, nursing care that just doesn't seem right. Most administrators and directors of nursing would want to know about problems like these. And approaching such concerns as a group can be a faster, more effective way to bring about change.

A word about laundry

One of the great nursing home mysteries involves personal laundry. Clothes disappear. Clothes are misplaced. Clothes are ruined. Plus, it takes more time than you ever imagined possible for clothes to come back from the laundry.

Some tips: Find out how long it takes for the facility to wash laundry and return it to residents' rooms, then do some math. Let's say the turnaround is four days. If your family member is incontinent, he or she may need two to four changes of clothes each day. So, you'll need to provide at least eight to sixteen changes of clothes. Assuming one or two episodes of incontinence per night, you will need four to eight changes of nightclothes. By providing enough clothes, you'll save yourself from running frequent loads of laundry at home.

Should you choose to do your loved one's laundry, post signs to that effect in his or her room and provide a container for the dirty clothes.

No matter who does the laundry, be sure to clearly mark each item with the resident's name and room number. That way, if clothing is moved or misplaced, it will stand a better chance of finding its way back to the right room. Also, the washers and dryers at the nursing home will wear out clothing faster than home washing, so you will need to replace clothes more often than usual.

Choose cheerful, comfortable clothing that is not only washable, but easy to put on and take off. Although your loved one may never have worn sweat suits before, they are warm, comfortable, and convenient in the nursing home. Extra socks and underwear are always needed, and comfortable, well-fitted shoes are essential to prevent tripping. Try sneakers with Velcro closures—they are easy to get on and off, and they fit snugly on the feet.

Working with nursing home staff

REMEMBER: WITHOUT STAFF, nothing is possible. To get the best from a nursing home, you need to work closely with staff members. Most nursing homes have many, many healthcare workers and other service providers caring for their residents. The organizational chart on the following page shows how all these providers work together.

Kinds of staff

The *nursing home administrator*, who oversees the entire nursing home, is responsible for all the residents and the staff. The administrator is licensed by the state to ensure that he or she understands the basics of the laws and regulations governing nursing homes, as well as the basics of geriatric care. The *director of nursing*, who is a registered nurse, oversees resident care and supervises all nurses, nursing assistants, and other care providers.

Most direct care is given by registered nurses (RNs), licensed practical or vocational nurses (LPNs or LVNs), and nursing assistants. *Registered nurses* have a minimum of two to four years' college education in nursing. They assess each resident, treat common medical problems, and see that every resident gets the care he or she needs. *Licensed practical nurses* and *licensed vocational nurses* have nine to twelve months' post-high-school education in basic nursing care. They are licensed to provide basic care and medical treatment to older adults.

Nursing assistants provide most of the "hands-on" care. Under the direction of licensed nurses, they assist residents with bathing, toileting, feeding, and more. Nursing assistants who work in a Medicare- or Medicaid-certified home are required to be certified themselves. This means they must complete a brief course of study on how to care for older adults, either before employment or within four months of beginning work in the nursing home, depending upon the state rules.

Nursing Home Staff

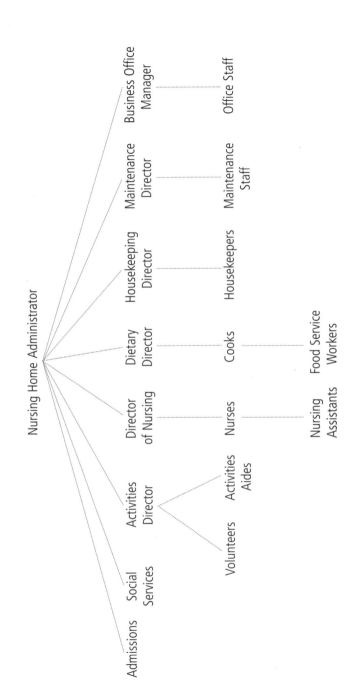

Other direct-care staff include social workers, activities directors, and dietary managers. Typically, a *social worker* will help new nursing home residents and their families through the admissions process. Social workers also help residents and families adjust to nursing home life, and they often arrange community services, such as Meals-on-Wheels, for people who are planning to return home after their nursing home stay.

The *activities director* not only organizes individual and group activities, but also recruits nursing home volunteers. *Volunteers* are essential to quality care—they read letters, assist with activities, and help keep the residents' lives rich and full.

"The activities person is a jewel. She can get my dad to do things I never thought he'd be willing to do."

It is the *dietary director's* job to ensure that meals are tasty and nutritious, offer a number of interesting choices, and are prepared the way the residents like them. The dietary director works with a dietitian to create balanced meals and address special dietary needs. He or she directs the dietary department, orders food and supplies, and oversees the cooks and other kitchen staff members during meal preparation.

Dietitians, pharmacists, and therapists also provide direct care, whether they are permanent staff members or independent contractors. *Dietitians* assess special dietary needs and help residents regain or maintain a healthy body weight. *Pharmacists* ensure that the medications residents take are appropriate for their condition. *Physical, occupational,* and *speech therapists* help residents regain functions lost due to illness or injury.

Finally, most nursing homes have business office staff to handle resident accounts, billing, insurance, payroll records, and employee paychecks. There may be one or several *maintenance workers* on staff to keep the heating, air conditioning, water, power, and building in good order, and to help residents with television hookup and room repairs. *Housekeepers* are assigned to all resident living units.

Educate staff about the resident

Nursing home staff members are just like anybody else—they tend to like people more as they get to know them better. As professionals, staff members should spend time getting to know each resident. You can help foster this relationship by telling the staff about key life details. For instance, what did you or your loved one enjoy before coming to live at the nursing home? What activities would be most enjoyable now? The more staff members know and understand about the people in their care, the easier it is for them to treat their residents with dignity and kindness.

Because nursing assistants provide most of the direct care, make a point of finding those assistants who have been there a while and get to know them well. But be warned: Many nursing assistants move frequently from job to job, so you'll need to continuously educate new staff members.

"It really helped to get to know the nursing assistants and the nurses well. I don't know what I would do without them. They have helped me so much with my mom."

A memory collage or a memory box can help the staff and other residents get to know you or your family member as a person—and both items are good for decorating a room. Include items that reflect earlier life. For example, a housewife and mother may include examples of needlework, a poem, pictures of her family, or a picture of herself as a young woman. A former firefighter may want to include citations for bravery, pictures of the crew, pictures of his family, or a miniature of his fire hat.

Make staff your ally

Communicating with the nursing home staff is vitally important to keeping the quality of care as high as possible. We recommend a tried-and-true method of communication: the Golden Rule. Treat others as you would want to be treated. As you get to know the staff, focus on building relationships that are strong, open, and respectful.

Naturally, problems will develop and the staff may well underestimate how much these difficulties disturb you. It's best to raise your concerns as problems occur. Be pleasant and respectful when speaking with the staff. Clearly identify your concerns in "I" words. For example, "I would appreciate it if you called me Mrs. Smith, not Ida. I have always been a very proper woman and I am not comfortable with people calling me by my first name." Or, "I noticed that Dad needs a haircut. When is he scheduled for the barber? He was always so meticulous about his hair." Of course, it's equally important to acknowledge when staff members are doing a good job: "I noticed how much extra care you took in explaining things to my mother. I really appreciate that. It will help her feel secure."

On occasion, the staff might behave in a way that makes you angry. Your strong reaction may be justified, but, unless you or your loved one are in danger, it is best not to confront others when you are angry. If you are too angry to have a reasonable discussion with the staff, stop. Often, a calmer approach will get you the results you want. Make an appointment with the administrator or the director of nursing, and try to remember that there is always more than one side to every story.

When preparing to discuss a problem with the nursing home staff, try this approach: First, identify what the real problem is. It may not be the most recent event, but one that happened three months ago that you didn't say anything about. Come to your meeting with facts, not just feelings. Be prepared to identify events, times, dates, and the personnel involved. Be ready to offer suggestions for improving the situation. At the end of the meeting, tell a key staff member that you would like the administrator to contact you when the situation has been resolved. Don't hesitate to contact the administrator or director of nursing again, if necessary.

Get to know the doctor

All nursing home residents have the right to choose their own healthcare provider; however, residents must select a provider who is a member of the facility's medical staff. The staff can provide a list of doctors to choose from.

The doctor may work closely with a nurse practitioner who specializes in the care of older people. Because both the doctor and nurse practitioner are an integral part of the nursing home team, it's important to maintain a good relationship with them. Stay engaged—if you ask questions, share information, and acknowledge good work, the physician or nurse practitioner will be more likely to answer your questions and respond to your requests in a timely manner.

If you feel that the doctor is not being helpful or does not work well with the nursing home staff, it may be best to choose another doctor at the facility.

The care plan

A CARE PLAN IS a written description of a resident's care. Think of the care plan as a road map that tells the staff how to reach specific care goals for you or your loved one. Goals that shape care plans may take several forms:

- *Improvement goals* identify a clinical situation that can be improved through care, such as recovery from a broken hip.
- *Maintenance goals* call for a plan to help maintain a resident's current level of functioning.
- *Preventive goals* identify ways to avoid a particular problem, such as complications of diabetes, for which a resident may be at risk.
- *Palliative goals* are used at the end of a person's life, when comfort is the highest priority.

Residents and their families are key to helping staff design and maintain individualized care plans. In cases where residents are confused, family members often have useful information—the resident's schedule before coming to the nursing home, medical problems, reactions to medications or treatments, early signs of illness—that the staff may need to be aware of.

Care planning needn't be formal. But it should be ongoing, since the resident's needs will change over time. Casual conversations with staff members can be quite helpful, as shared information is often used to improve care. However, the staff may not always appear to value your input. If you believe that you are offering important information, insist that it be added to the care plan and other permanent records.

The federal government mandates quarterly care-plan reviews for each resident. By law, residents and their family members may attend these reviews. The care-plan review is your best opportunity to communicate key needs and wishes to the staff.

Although the structure and formality of these meetings may vary, care-plan reviews often involve many members of the nursing home team—a nurse assessment coordinator, activities director, social worker, nurse, dietary manager or dietitian, and various therapists. Physicians are not usually present due to scheduling complications and reimbursement policies. (Medicare limits payments to physicians for the care of nursing home residents, just as it limits payments for office visits.)

At the meeting, staff members will review the care plan and coordinate efforts to reach each resident's goals. If a resident has a problem with depression and weight loss, for instance, the dietitian may suggest adding nutritional supplements; the social worker may recall the family's willingness to bring in a favorite bedtime snack; the nurse may suggest contacting the pharmacist and physician to change the antidepressant medication; the activities director may plan to be more persistent when inviting the resident to group activities.

Although the care-plan conference is a time for group problem-solving, it is generally too brief—families get only

10 to 15 minutes each—for you to air all your concerns. It's best to address most concerns with staff before the meeting. Also, be sure to read the care plan ahead of time—it will give you an idea of what kinds of care the staff has planned for you or your loved one.

Care plans often are not individualized enough, but you can help change this by offering suggestions that can only come from you. For example, "Mom would never do crafts, but she is very religious and will likely go to a Bible meeting or other church group. Please see that she goes at least three times each week." If you or your resident have specific ideas for improving care, see that they are noted in the plan.

"You know, I just need someone to help me take care of myself. I want the place really clean, and this is. And I want good food, and we have that. Good food, nice place, and they help take care of me, too."

Follow up on the care plan

State and federal regulations require nursing homes to create and follow care plans. Your job is to regularly review your plan, ask pertinent questions, and request any changes that might make it more effective.

Follow up on your requests. It's frustrating, but you may have to request something more than once before it gets done consistently. Don't give up. Ask that your request be added to the care plan or noted somewhere that staff members are likely to see it. For instance, if you or your loved one prefer card games to bingo, insist that staff members offer activities other than bingo.

Nursing home surveys

When the nursing home asks you to fill out a satisfaction survey, it's important to respond; your answers may influence future nursing home policy. Surveys generally go to both residents and family members. Often, family members who help their resident complete the survey are surprised by their loved one's answers.

If you would like to see the survey results, ask the administrator or social worker.

7

Ombudsmen, Agencies, and Web Sites

Nursing home residents have access to an ombudsman, a consumer advocate who investigates and attempts to resolve residents' concerns and complaints. The ombudsman in your area may be able to help you in your search for a good nursing home. He or she will be familiar with many homes in your state and can discuss issues of concern to nursing home residents and their families. On the following pages you will find a state-by-state list of ombudsman programs. You will also find a list of state licensure and certifications programs, as well as a directory of web sites to help you in your nursing home search.

Ombudsman programs

Alabama

State Long-Term Care Ombudsman
Alabama Department of Senior Services
770 Washington Avenue
RSA Plaza, Suite 470
Montgomery, Alabama 36130
(334) 242-5743
fax: (334) 242-5594

Alaska

State Long-Term Care Ombudsman
Alaska Commission on Aging
3601 C Street, Suite 260
Anchorage, Alaska 99503-5209
(907) 334-4480
in-state: (800) 730-6393
fax: (907) 334-4486

Arizona

State Long-Term Care Ombudsman
Aging and Adult Administration
Department of Economic Security
1789 W. Jefferson Street, 950A
Phoenix, Arizona 85007
(602) 542-4446
fax: (602) 542-6575

Arkansas

State Long-Term Care Ombudsman
Division of Aging and Adult Services
Arkansas Department of Human Services
P.O. Box 1437, Slot 1412
Little Rock, Arkansas 72203-1437
(501) 682-2441
fax: (501) 682-8155

California

State Long-Term Care Ombudsman
Department of Aging
1600 K Street
Sacramento, California 95814
(916) 322-5290
fax: (916) 323-7299

Colorado

State Long-Term Care Ombudsman
The Legal Center
455 Sherman Street, Suite 130
Denver, Colorado 80203
(303) 722-0300
fax: (303) 722-0720

Connecticut

State Long-Term Care Ombudsman
Elderly Services Division
25 Sigourney Street, 10th Floor
Hartford, Connecticut 06106-5033
(860) 424-5200
fax: (860) 424-4966

Delaware

State Long-Term Care Ombudsman
Division of Services for the Aging and Adults
with Physical Disabilities
1901 N. DuPont Highway
New Castle, Delaware 19720
(302) 577-4791
fax: (302) 577-4793

District of Columbia

Long-Term Care Ombudsman for the District of Columbia
Legal Counsel for the Elderly, AARP Foundation
601 E Street N.W.
Washington, DC 20049
(202) 434-2120
fax: (202) 434-6595

Florida

State Long-Term Care Ombudsman
LTC Ombudsman Counsel
600 S. Calhoun Street, Suite 270
Tallahassee, Florida 32301
(850) 488-6190
fax: (850) 488-5657

Georgia

State Long-Term Care Ombudsman
Division of Aging Services
Two Peachtree Street N.W., 36th Floor
Atlanta, Georgia 30303-3176
(404) 463-8383
(888) 454-5826
fax: (404) 657-5285

Hawaii

State Long-Term Care Ombudsman
Executive Office on Aging
250 S. Hotel Street, Suite 109
Honolulu, Hawaii 96813-2831
(808) 586-0100
fax: (808) 586-0185

Idaho

State Long-Term Care Ombudsman
Commission on Aging
P.O. Box 83720
Boise, Idaho 83720-0007
(208) 334-3833
fax: (208) 334-3033

Illinois

State Long-Term Care Ombudsman
Illinois Department on Aging
421 E. Capitol Avenue, Suite 100
Springfield, Illinois 62701-1789
(217) 524-6911
in-state (800) 252-8966
fax: (217) 524-9644

Indiana

State Long-Term Care Ombudsman
Aging and Rehabilitation Services
P.O. Box 7083-W454
402 W. Washington Street, Room W-454
Indianapolis, Indiana 46204-7083
(317) 232-7134
fax: (317) 232-7867
fax: (317) 233-2182

Iowa

State Long-Term Care Ombudsman
Department of Elder Affairs
200 Tenth Street, 3rd Floor
Clemens Building
Des Moines, Iowa 50309-3609
(515) 242-3328
fax: (515) 242-3300

Kansas

State Long-Term Care Ombudsman
610 S.W. Tenth Avenue, Second Floor
Topeka, Kansas 66612-1616
(785) 296-3017
fax: (785) 296-3916

Kentucky

State Long-Term Care Ombudsman
Office of Aging Services
275 E. Main Street
Frankfort, Kentucky 40621
(502) 564-6930
fax: (502) 564-4595

Louisiana

State Long-Term Care Ombudsman
Governor's Office of Elderly Affairs
412 N. Fourth Street, 3rd Floor
Baton Rouge, Louisiana 70802
(225) 342-7100
in-state: (800) 259-4990
fax: (225) 342-7144

Maine

State Long-Term Care Ombudsman
P.O. Box 128
Augusta, Maine 04332
(207) 621-1079
fax: (207) 621-0509

Maryland

State Long-Term Care Ombudsman
Maryland Department of Aging
301 W. Preston Street, Room 1004
Baltimore, Maryland 21201
(410) 767-1100
fax: (410) 333-7943

Massachusetts

State Long-Term Care Ombudsman
Commonwealth of Massachusetts
Executive Office of Elder Affairs
One Ashburton Place, 5th Floor
Boston, Massachusetts 02108-1518
(617) 727-7750
fax: (617) 727-9368

Michigan

State Long-Term Care Ombudsman
Citizens for Better Care
4750 Woodward Avenue, Suite 410
Detroit, Michigan 48201-1308
(313) 832-6387
fax: (313) 832-7407

Minnesota

State Long-Term Care Ombudsman
Office of Ombudsman for Older Minnesotans
121 E. Seventh Place, Suite 280
St. Paul, Minnesota 55101
(651) 296-0382
fax: (651) 297-5654

Mississippi

State Long-Term Care Ombudsman
Division of Aging and Adult Services
750 N. State Street
Jackson, Mississippi 39202
(601) 359-4929
fax: (601) 359-9664

Missouri

State Long-Term Care Ombudsman
Department of Social Services
Division of Aging
P.O. Box 1337
Jefferson City, Missouri 65102
(573) 526-0727
(800) 309-3282
fax: (573) 751-8687

Montana

State Long-Term Care Ombudsman
Office on Aging
Senior and Long-Term Care Division
Department of Public Health and Human Services
P.O. Box 4210
Helena, Montana 59604-4210
(406) 444-4077
fax: (406) 444-7743

Nebraska

State Long-Term Care Ombudsman
Department of Health and Human Services
Division of Aging and Disability Services
P.O. Box 95044
Lincoln, Nebraska 68509-5044
(402) 471-2307
fax: (402) 471-4619

Nevada

State Long-Term Care Ombudsman
Department of Human Resources
Division for Aging Services
340 N. Eleventh Street, Suite 203
Las Vegas, Nevada 89101
(702) 486-3545
fax: (702) 486-3572

New Hampshire

State Long-Term Care Ombudsman
Health and Human Services
129 Pleasant Street
Concord, New Hampshire 03301-6505
(603) 271-4375
fax: (603) 271-4771

New Jersey

State Long-Term Care Ombudsman
Office of the Ombudsman for the Institutionalized Elderly
P.O. Box 807
Trenton, New Jersey 08625-0807
(609) 588-3614
fax: (609) 588-3365

New Mexico

State Long-Term Care Ombudsman
State Agency on Aging
228 E. Palace Avenue
Santa Fe, New Mexico 87501
(505) 827-7640
fax: (505) 827-7649

New York

State Long-Term Care Ombudsman
New York State Office for the Aging
Two Empire State Plaza
Albany, New York 12223-0001
(518) 474-0108
fax: (518) 474-7761

North Carolina

State Long-Term Care Ombudsman
Division of Aging
2101 Mail Service Center
Raleigh, North Carolina 27699-2101
(919) 733-3983
fax: (919) 715-0868

North Dakota

State Long-Term Care Ombudsman
Department of Health and Human Services
Aging Services Division
600 S. Second Street, Suite 1C
Bismarck, North Dakota 58504
(701) 328-8910
fax: (701) 328-8989

Ohio

State Long-Term Care Ombudsman
Ohio Department of Aging
50 W. Broad Street, 9th Floor
Columbus, Ohio 43215-3363
(614) 466-1221
(800) 282-1206
fax: (614) 466-5741

Oklahoma

State Long-Term Care Ombudsman
Aging Services Division
Department of Human Services
312 N.E. Twenty-Eighth Street
Oklahoma City, Oklahoma 73105
(405) 521-6734
fax: (405) 521-2086

Oregon

State Long-Term Care Ombudsman
3855 Wolverine N.E., Suite 6
Salem, Oregon 97305-1251
(503) 378-6533
fax: (503) 373-0852

Pennsylvania

State Long-Term Care Ombudsman
Pennsylvania Department of Aging
555 Walnut Street, 5th Floor
Harrisburg, Pennsylvania 17101-1919
(717) 783-7247
fax: (717) 772-3382

The New Nursing Homes

Rhode Island

State Long-Term Care Ombudsman
Alliance for Better Long-Term Care
422 Post Road, Suite 204
Warwick, Rhode Island 02888
(401) 785-3340
fax: (401) 785-3391

South Carolina

State Long-Term Care Ombudsman
Division on Aging
1801 Main Street
P.O. Box 8206
Columbia, South Carolina 29202-8206
(803) 898-2580
fax: (803) 898-4513

South Dakota

State Long-Term Care Ombudsman
Department of Social Services
Office of Adult Services and Aging
700 Governors Drive
Pierre, South Dakota 57501-2291
(605) 773-3656
fax: (605) 773-6834

Tennessee

State Long-Term Care Ombudsman
Commission on Aging
500 Deaderick Street, 9th Floor
Nashville, Tennessee 37243-0860
(615) 741-2056
fax: (615) 741-3309

Texas

State Long-Term Care Ombudsman
Texas Department on Aging
4900 N. Lamar Boulevard
Austin, Texas 78751
(512) 424-6875
fax: (512) 424-6890

Utah

State Long-Term Care Ombudsman
Aging and Adult Services
120 North 200 W., Room 325
Salt Lake City, Utah 84103
(801) 538-3910
fax: (801) 538-4395

Vermont

State Long-Term Care Ombudsman
Vermont Legal Aid, Inc.
P.O. Box 1367
264 N. Winooski Avenue
Burlington, Vermont 05402
(802) 863-5620
fax: (802) 863-7152

Virginia

State Long-Term Care Ombudsman
Virginia Association of Area Agencies on Aging
530 E. Main Street, Suite 428
Richmond, Virginia 23219
(804) 644-2923
fax: (804) 644-5640

Washington

State Long-Term Care Ombudsman
South King County Multi-Services Center
P.O. Box 23699
1200 S. 336th Street
Federal Way, Washington 98093-7699
in-state (800) 562-6028
(253) 838-6810
fax: (253) 815-8173

West Virginia

State Long-Term Care Ombudsman
West Virginia Bureau of Senior Services
Commission on Aging
1900 Kanawha Boulevard E.
Holly Grove Building 10
Charleston, West Virginia 25305-0160
(304) 558-3317
fax: (304) 558-0004

Wisconsin

State Long-Term Care Ombudsman
Board on Aging and Long-Term Care
214 N. Hamilton Street
Madison, Wisconsin 53703-2118
(800) 815-0015
fax: (608) 261-6570

Wyoming

State Long-Term Care Ombudsman
Wyoming Long-Term Care Ombudsman Program
P.O. Box 94
Wheatland, Wyoming 82201
(307) 322-5553
fax: (307) 322-3283

State licensure and certification programs

ALL NURSING HOMES are licensed by the state in which they are located. Homes that participate in Medicaid or Medicare must also be certified by the state agency responsible for nursing home regulation. The following list of state licensure and certification programs may be useful in your nursing home search, or if you have questions after moving into a nursing home.

Alabama

Executive Director
Division of Provider Services
Department of Public Health
P.O. Box 303017
Montgomery, Alabama 36130-3017
(334) 206-5175
fax: (334) 206-5219

Alaska

Director
Health Facilities Licensing and Certification
Department of Health and Social Services
4730 Business Park Boulevard, Suite 18
Building H
Anchorage, Alaska 50399-503
(907) 561-8081
fax: (907) 561-3011

Arizona

Program Director
Division of Assurance and Licensure Services
Arizona Department of Human Services
1647 E. Morten Avenue, Suite 130
Phoenix, Arizona 85020-4610
(602) 674-9705
fax: (602) 395-8910

Arkansas

Director
Division of Medical Services
Office of Long-Term Care
Arkansas Department of Human Services
P.O. Box 8059, Mail Slot 400
Little Rock, Arkansas 72203-8059
(501) 682-8430
fax: (501) 682-6955

California

Deputy Director
Licensing and Certification Program
Department of Health Services
P.O. Box 942732
1800 Third Street, Suite 210
Sacramento, California 94234-7320
(916) 445-3054
fax: (916) 324-1054

Colorado

Director
Health Facilities Division
Colorado Department of Public Health and Environment
4300 Cherry Creek Drive S.
Denver, Colorado 80246
(303) 692-2835
fax: (303) 782-4883

Connecticut

Director
State of Connecticut Department of Public Health
410 Capitol Avenue, Mail Slot 12HSR
P.O. Box 340308
Hartford, Connecticut 06134
(860) 509-7406
fax: (860) 509-7538

Delaware

Director
Division of Long-Term Care Residents Protection
Delaware Department of Health and Social Services
3 Mill Road, Suite 308
Wilmington, Delaware 19806
(302) 577-6666
fax: (302) 577-6672

District of Columbia

Director
Health Regulation Administration
Department of Health
825 N. Capitol Street, N.E.
Washington, DC 20002
(202) 442-5888
fax: (202) 442-9430

Florida

Secretary
Long-Term Care Unit
Florida Agency for Health Care
Mail Station 33
2727 Mahan Drive
Tallahassee, Florida 32308
(850) 448-5861
fax: (850) 410-1512

Georgia

Director
Office of Regulatory Service of Long-Term Care
Department of Human Resources
Two Peachtree Street N.W., Suite 31-447
Atlanta, Georgia 30303
(404) 657-5850
fax: (404) 657-8935

Hawaii

Director
Office of Health Care Assurance
Department of Health
State of Hawaii
P.O. Box 3378
Honolulu, Hawaii 96801
(808) 586-4080
fax: (808) 692-7447

Idaho

Director
Bureau of Facility Standards
P.O. Box 83720
Boise, Idaho 83720-0036
(208) 334-6626
fax: (208) 364-1888

Illinois

Director
Office of Quality Assurance
Illinois Department of Public Health
525–535 W. Jefferson Street
Springfield, Illinois 62761-0001
(217) 782-5180
fax: (217) 524-0529

Indiana

Director
Mail Stop 21-10
Bureau of Aging and In-Home Services
P.O. Box 7083
402 W. Washington Street, Room W-454
Indianapolis, Indiana 46204-7083
(317) 232-7020
fax: (317) 232-7867

Iowa

Executive Director
Health Facilities Division
Department of Inspections and Appeals
Lucas State Office Building
Des Moines, Iowa 50319-0083
(515) 281-4115
fax: (515) 242-5022

Kansas

Secretary
Health Facilities
Landon State Office Building
900 S.W. Jackson, Suite 1001
Topeka, Kansas 66612
(785) 296-1240
fax: (785) 296-1266

Kentucky

Director
Licensing and Regulation
Office of the Inspector General
275 E. Main Street, Mail Stop SE
Frankfort, Kentucky 40621
(502) 564-6786
fax: (502) 564-6546

Louisiana

Director
State of Louisiana Health Standards
P.O. Box 3767
Baton Rouge, Louisiana 70821-3767
(225) 342-0138
fax: (225) 342-5292

Maine

Director
Bureau of Medical Services
Division of Licensing and Certification
Department of Human Services
35 Anthony Avenue
11 State House Station
Augusta, Maine 04333-0011
(207) 624-5443
fax: (207) 624-5378

Maryland

Secretary
Office of Health Care Quality
Spring Grove Hospital Center
BB Building
55 Wade Avenue
Baltimore, Maryland 21228
(410) 402-8000
fax: (410) 402-8234

Massachusetts

Secretary
Licensure and Certification
Division of Health Care Quality
10 West Street, 5th Floor
Boston, Massachusetts 02111
(617) 753-8000
fax: (617) 753-8095

Michigan

Director
MDCIS
Bureau of Health Systems
Division of Nursing Home Monitoring
P.O. Box 30664
Lansing, Michigan 48909
(517) 241-2506
fax: (517) 241-2629

Minnesota

Executive Secretary
Long-Term Care and Certification
Division of Facility and Provider Compliance
85 E. Seventh Place, Suite 300
St. Paul, Minnesota 57101
(651) 215-8701
fax: (651) 215-8709

Mississippi

Director
Licensure and Certification
570 E. Woodrow Wilson, Suite 200
Jackson, Mississippi 39215
(601) 576-7300
fax: (601) 576-7208

Missouri

Director
Division of Aging
615 Howerton Court
P.O. Box 1337
Jefferson City, Missouri 65102
(573) 751-3082
fax: (573) 751-8687

Montana

State Aging Coordinator
Quality Assurance Division
Department of Public Health and Human Services
2401 Colonial Drive
Helena, Montana 59620
(406) 444-2031
fax: (406) 444-1742
fax: (406) 444-3456

Nebraska

Administrator
Regulation and Licensure
Credentialing Division
Department of Health and Human Services
301 Centennial Mall S.
P.O. Box 95007
Lincoln, Nebraska 68509-5007
(402) 471-2946
fax: (402) 471-0555

Nevada

Administrator
Bureau of Licensure and Certification
1550 E. College Parkway, Suite 158
Carson City, Nevada 89706
(775) 687-4475
fax: (775) 687-6588

New Hampshire

Director
Office of Program Support
Health Facilities Administration
Department of Health and Human Services
129 Pleasant Street
Concord, New Hampshire 03301-3857
(603) 271-4592
fax: (603) 271-4968

New Jersey

Assistant Commissioner
Division of Long-Term Care Systems
New Jersey Department of Health Services
P.O. Box 367
Trenton, New Jersey 08625
(609) 633-9034
fax: (609) 633-9087

New Mexico

Director
Health Facilities Licensing and Certification Bureau
525 Camino de los Marquez, Suite 2
Santa Fe, New Mexico 87501
(505) 827-7640
fax: (505) 827-2403

New York

Executive Director
Office of Continuing Care
New York State Department of Health
166 Delaware Avenue
Delmar, New York 12054
(518) 474-1000
fax: (518) 474-1134

North Carolina

Director
Division of Facilities Services
Licensure and Certification Section
Department of Health and Human Services
2711 Mail Service Center
Raleigh, North Carolina 27699-2711
(919) 733-7461
fax: (919) 733-8274

North Dakota

Director
Division of Health Facilities
North Dakota Department of Health
600 E. Boulevard Avenue
Bismarck, North Dakota 58505-0200
(701) 328-2352
fax: (701) 328-1890

Ohio

Director
Licensure Program
Ohio Department of Health
246 N. High Street
Columbus, Ohio 43215-2412
(614) 466-7713
fax: (614) 752-4157

Oklahoma

Division Administrator
Special Health Services
Oklahoma State Health Department
1000 N.E. Tenth Street
Oklahoma City, Oklahoma 73117
(405) 271-6868
fax: (405) 271-3442

Oregon

Administrator
Long-Term Care Quality Section
Senior and Disabled Services Division
500 Summer Street N.E.
Salem, Oregon 97310
(503) 945-5853
fax: (503) 947-5046

Pennsylvania

Secretary
Bureau of Facility Licensure and Certification
Division of Nursing Care Facilities
Pennsylvania Department of Health
Room 526, Health and Welfare Building
Harrisburg, Pennsylvania 17120
(717) 787-1816
fax: (717) 772-2163

Rhode Island

Director
Rhode Island Department of Health
Division of Facilities Regulation
3 Capitol Hill, Room 306
Providence, Rhode Island 09908
(401) 222-2566
fax: (401) 222-6548

South Carolina

Office of Senior and Long-Term Care Services
Division of Health Licensing
Department of Health and Environmental Control
2600 Bull Street
Columbia, South Carolina 29201-8206
(803) 737-7370
fax: (803) 737-7212

South Dakota

Administrator
Licensure and Certification
South Dakota Department of Health
615 E. Fourth Street
Pierre, South Dakota 57501-1700
(605) 773-3357
fax: (605) 773-6667

Tennessee

Executive Director
Office of Health Licensure and Regulation
Division of Health Care Facilities
Tennessee Department of Health
425 Fifth Avenue N.
Cordell Hull Building, 1st Floor
Nashville, Tennessee 37247
(615) 741-7221
fax: (615) 741-7051

Texas

Executive Director
Long-Term Care Regulatory, Mail Code E-342
Texas Department of Human Services
P.O. Box 149030
Austin, Texas 78714-9030
(512) 438-2633
in-state: (800) 458-9858
fax: (512) 438-2722

Utah

Director
Bureau of Licensing
Department of Health
288 North 1460 West
P.O. Box 142003
Salt Lake City, Utah 84116
(801) 538-6152
fax: (801) 538-6325

Vermont

Commissioner
Division of Licensing and Protection
Department of Aging and Disabilities
103 S. Main Street, Ladd Hall
Waterbury, Vermont 05671-2306
(802) 241-2345
fax: (802) 241-2358

Virginia

Commissioner
Division of Long-Term Care Services
Center for Quality Health Care Services and
Consumer Protection
Virginia State Department of Health
3600 W. Broad Street, Suite 216
Richmond, Virginia 23230-4920
(804) 367-2100
fax: (804) 367-2149

Washington

Assistant Secretary
Residential Care Services
Department of Social and Health Services
P.O. Box 45600
Olympia, Washington 98504-5600
(360) 725-2300
fax: (360) 407-0369

West Virginia

Commissioner
Licensure and Certification
Office of Health Facilities
350 Capitol Street, Room 206
Charleston, West Virginia 25301-3718
(304) 558-0050
fax: (304) 558-2515

Wisconsin

Director
Bureau of Quality Assurance
Department of Health and Family Services
One W. Wilson Street, Room 950
Madison, Wisconsin 53701
(608) 266-8847
fax: (608) 267-7119

Wyoming

Administrator
Office of Health Quality
Department of Health
2020 Carey Avenue, 8th Floor
Cheyenne, Wyoming 82002
(307) 777-7123
fax: (307) 777-7127

Helpful web sites

OF THE HUNDREDS OF web sites covering care and services for the elderly, we've handpicked a few of the best. These sites cover nursing home care, financing, annual inspection results, advocacy organizations, and more.

State and federal agencies compile information about each resident living in a Medicare- or Medicaid-certified home. They document problems like weight loss, dehydration, skin breakdown, behavior problems, falls, fractures, and more. In the near future, one of the federal web sites will summarize this information and list "quality indicators" scores for nursing homes around the country. This will enable consumers to easily compare scores for each nursing home in their state.

Quality indicators scores range from 0 to 100, with 0 being the best. You will need to interpret these scores carefully—they may indicate potential problems that require further investigation. The scores are designed to help state and federal survey agencies spot problems, and to help nursing home staff improve their quality of service. Quality indicators may or may not be an accurate reflection of nursing home quality; they simply provide another piece of information for consumers. Watch for these reports on the Internet in the near future.

Also, the Administration on Aging web site has links to state Area Agencies on Aging. These agencies coordinate senior services and eldercare information in each state. If you anticipate a short stay in the nursing home, you may want to contact your local Area Agency on Aging to ask about community services that might help after you or your resident return home.

Administration on Aging

http://www.aoa.dhhs.gov/agingsites/default.htm
Links to state Area Agencies on Aging, federal agency consumer web sites, and other resources.

American Association of Homes and Services for the Aging

http://www.aahsa.org
Links to the organization's state associations.

American Health Care Association

http://www.ahca.org
Links to the organization's state associations.

ElderWeb

http://www.elderweb.com/about.htm
Contains information about eldercare topics, state-specific Medicaid regulations, and more.

Health Care Financing Administration

http://www.hcfa.gov

Offers information about federal regulations, quality care initiatives, Medicare, and Medicaid.

Murphy's Unofficial Medicaid page

http://www.geocites.com/CapitolHill/5974

A resource guide to Medicaid. Offers information about Medicaid-specific resources and links to state-specific Medicaid sites.

National Aging Information Center

http://www.aoa.dhhs.gov/NAIC/Notes/default.htm

Links to major web resources on topics related to aging.

National Citizens' Coalition for Nursing Home Reform

http://www.nccnhr.org

The national advocacy group that defines and improves quality long-term care. This site offers links to state advocacy groups.

Nursing Home Compare: The Health Care Financing Administration's Nursing Home Search

http://www.medicare.gov/NHCompare/home.asp

The Health Care Financing Administration's (HCFA) nursing home database includes information about every Medicare- and Medicaid-certified nursing home in the United States, and whether they have complied with nursing home regulations.

About the Authors

Marilyn Rantz, RN, PhD, NHA, FAAN
Professor, Sinclair School of Nursing
University Hospitals Professor of Nursing
Chair of MU MDS and Quality Research Team
University of Missouri-Columbia

DR. MARILYN RANTZ is recognized as the country's leading expert on quality of care in nursing homes. She is a licensed nursing home administrator who, for many years, supervised a large county nursing home in southern Wisconsin, which was renowned for its excellent care and services. For years she has conducted quality of care research, consulting widely in the United States and abroad on how to improve the care of older adults.

Currently, Dr. Rantz chairs the University of Missouri-Columbia Minimum Data Set (MDS) and Quality Research Team. She heads multiple research projects focused on understanding and improving the quality of services available for older adults. She is a fellow in the American Academy of Nursing. She is also the author of almost one hundred articles or book chapters, as well as several books on quality improvement, health policy, nursing diagnosis, quality assurance, nursing management, and care of the elderly. Two books that she coauthored have earned Book of the Year Awards from the American Journal of Nursing (AJN): *Quality of Health Care for Older People in America: A Review of Nursing Studies* (American Nurses Association, 1991) and *Outcome-Based Quality Improvement for Long-Term Care: Using MDS, Process, and*

Outcome Measures (Aspen Publishing, 1998). Another book, *Using MDS Quality Indicators to Improve Outcomes* (Aspen Publishing, 1998) has been used extensively by quality improvement teams to evaluate nursing homes and improve care.

Dr. Rantz is committed to helping families find the best nursing homes. "There are good nursing homes, ones with progressive care ideas. The trick is finding them and knowing what to look for. Our walk-through questions have been field-tested and found to be extremely helpful to families who face this frequently guilt-ridden decision. Using the walk-through to objectively find the best possible care has helped families and residents view the nursing home as a blessing in a time of need, rather than a terrifying experience."

Lori Popejoy, RN, MSN, CS, GCNS
Gerontological Clinical Nurse Specialist
Director of Clinical Services
University Nurses Senior Care
Sinclair School of Nursing
University of Missouri-Columbia

MS. POPEJOY IS ONE of the country's leading clinical experts in the care of older adults. An ANCC-certified Gerontological Clinical Nurse Specialist, she consults widely with nursing homes to help them improve care and services. For several years, she was the long-term care research nurse consultant of the MU MDS and Quality Research Team. She worked with nursing homes throughout Missouri to improve resident outcomes using MDS quality indicator data. She frequently speaks on topics related to the MDS and to quality indicators derived from MDS data. She is coauthor of two books: *Using MDS Quality Indicators to Improve Outcomes* (Aspen Publishing, 1998) and *Outcome-Based Quality Improvement for Long-Term Care: Using MDS, Process, and Outcome Measures* (Aspen Publishing, 1998), which won an AJN Book of the Year Award.

She is currently director of clinical services for University Nurses Senior Care, a new model for community-based care to help older adults "age in place" in the housing of their choice.

Ms. Popejoy is committed to helping older adults and their families find the best possible nursing home when they need it. She explains, "People often think that being at home is the best thing for someone who needs a lot of help and care. But home may mean isolation and limited help. I think of Elsie. She was a lovely, blind eighty-year-old woman who for years feared to go out of her house because she thought she might spill something on her clothes and look bad. After her husband died and she moved into the nursing home, she became social again. Activities staff convinced her to come with them to Kmart—it was her first outing in years. She went out to eat with friends, something she would not do before learning to eat with the other residents in the nursing home. Then, she insisted that she needed a beautiful robe, a 'drop-dead duster,' as she put it, to wear to breakfast with the people she met on her floor. You know, she never needed a 'drop-dead duster' when she was isolated at home. Because her friends helped her find the best nursing home they could, her life was good and full until the end at age eighty-nine."

Mary Zwygart-Stauffacher, RN, PhD, CS, GNP/GCNS
Professor and Chair, Department of Nursing Systems
School of Nursing
University of Wisconsin-Eau Claire
and
Gerontological Nurse Practitioner
Red Cedar Clinic/Mayo Health System
Menomonie, Wisconsin

DR. ZWYGART-STAUFFACHER is one of the country's leading experts in the care of older adults. She is widely recognized not only for her research expertise, but also her clinical skills with nursing home residents. In addition to her faculty role at the University of Wisconsin-Eau Claire, she has a primary care practice with physicians managing residents in several nursing homes. For more than twenty years, she has worked as a gerontological nurse in many teaching, consulting, and practice positions. She is a former JCAHO surveyor for the long-term care division, and is presently a member of a technical expert panel for the federal Health Care Financing Administration (HCFA) Skilled Nursing Facility Prospective Payment System Quality Medical Review Project. She has consulted with numerous nursing schools about gerontological nursing curricula and nurse practitioner education. She has also consulted with many nursing homes about quality of care issues and program development.

Dr. Zwygart-Stauffacher is a sought-after collaborator on nursing home research projects, particularly those examining quality of care. She has authored numerous publications and coauthored *Outcome-Based Quality Improvement for Long-Term*

Care: Using MDS, Process, and Outcome Measures (Aspen Publishing, 1998), which won an AJN Book of the Year Award. Dr. Zwygart-Stauffacher explains, "Coming to the nursing home, while a stressful move for some people, can be a positive thing. When people need care, and you find a good nursing home to provide that care, some residents feel relieved that they now have help and are no longer struggling on their own. Some older adults feel that they are safe for the first time in a long while. Nursing home care can be the best thing for some people. I am concerned about how society can make families feel guilty for not providing all the care that some older adults need. Sometimes, the care is just too much, and the need for it goes on too long for families to do it all themselves."

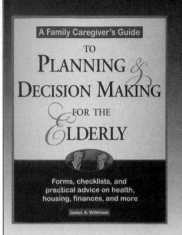